P · O · C · K · E · T · S

HORSES

BURCHELL'S ZEBRA

12TH CENTURY
STIRRUP IRON

ARABIAN
CIRCUS
HORSE

RIDING HORSE

P · O · C · K · E · T · S

HORSES

Written by
DAVID ALDERTON

Donkey
and trap

Mounted
police officer

Shire
horse

Shetland
pony

A DORLING KINDERSLEY BOOK

Project editor Alan Burrows
Art editor Carole Oliver
Senior editor Laura Buller
Senior art editor Helen Senior
Picture research Anna Lord
Production Louise Barratt
US editor Jill Hamilton
US consultant Sharon Ralls Lemon

First American edition, 1995
6 8 10 9 7 5
Published in the United States by
DK Publishing Inc., 95 Madison Avenue
New York, New York 10016

Visit us on the World Wide Web at http://www.dk.com

Library of Congress Cataloging-in-Publication Data
Alderton, David. 1956-
  Horses / by David Alderton – 1st American ed.
  p. cm. – (A DK pocket)
  Includes index.
  ISBN 1-56458-890-4
  1. Horses–Juvenile literature. [1. Horses] I. Title. II. Series
SF302.A38 1995
636.1–dc20   94-31844
                                                    CIP
                                                    AC

Color reproduction by Colourscan, Singapore
Printed and bound in Italy by L.E.G.O.

CONTENTS

How to use this book 8

INTRODUCTION TO HORSES 10

What is a horse? 12

The horse in history 14

The first horses 18

Main horse types 20

Body and conformation 22

Coat colors 26

Movement 30

Food and diet 32

Behavior 34

Life cycle of a horse 36

Uses of the horse 40

Horse riding 44

PONIES 48

Introduction to ponies 50

Shetland 52

Highland 54

Fell and Dales 56

Exmoor and Dartmoor 58

New Forest Pony 60
Welsh Mountain Pony and Australian Pony 62
Connemara 64
Chincoteague 66
Haflinger 68
Caspian 70
Falabella 72
Icelandic Horse 74

LIGHT HORSES 76
Introduction to light horses 78
Barb 80
Thoroughbred 82
Pinto and Palomino 84
Arab 86
Quarter Horse 88
Appaloosa 90
Andalucian 92
Cleveland Bay 94
Trakehner 96
Lipizzaner 98
Australian Stock Horse 100
Morgan and Dutch Warmblood 102

HEAVY HORSES 104
Introduction to heavy horses 106
Jutland 108
Brabant 110
Percheron 112
Clydesdale 114
Suffolk Punch 116

Shire 118
Ardennais 120

WILD AND FERAL HORSES 122
Introduction to wild and feral horses 124
Przewalski's Horse 126
Zebra 128
Ass, donkey, mule, and hinny 130
Feral horses 132

REFERENCE SECTION 134
Classification 136
Records and facts 138
Learning to ride 140
Choosing a horse 144
Horse care 146
Drawing a horse 150

Resources 152
Glossary 154
Index 156

How to use this book

These pages show you how to use *Pockets: Horses*.
The book is divided into several sections. The main
sections consist of information on different breeds of
horse. There is also an introductory section at the
front, and a reference section at the back. Each new
section begins with a picture page, which gives an
idea of what it is about.

HORSE TYPES
The horses in the book are arranged
into four main types: ponies, light
horses, heavy horses, and wild and
feral horses. Each type features
recognized breeds. Often, other
breeds, which are considered as
influences, are also included.

Corner coding

Heading

Introduction

LIGHT HORSES

CLEVELAND BAY
DESCENDED FROM THE English Yorkshire Coach
Horses of the 1800s, these versatile workers pull
royal carriage on state occasions. The horses are
called Cleveland Bays
because they originally
came from Cleveland on
the northeastern coast of
England. They are
characterized by a
distinctive bay-
colored coat with a
black mane and tail.

Curved and
graceful neck

Muscular neck
and sloping
shoulders
provide power

ROYAL CARRIAGE HORSES
The Cleveland Bays used in England to pull the
royal carriages are kept in the Royal Mews near
Buckingham Palace in London. At one time, the
Duke of Edinburgh raced a team of part Cleveland
Bays in driving competitions.

No feathers
on the heels

94

Size indicator

CORNER CODING
Corners of horse and
pony pages are color
coded with yellow, blue,
red, and green to
remind you which
section you are in.

☐ PONIES
☐ LIGHT HORSES
☐ HEAVY HORSES
☐ WILD AND
FERAL HORSES

HEADING
This describes the
subject of the page.
This page is about the
Cleveland Bay. If a
subject continues over
several pages, the
same heading applies.

INTRODUCTION
This provides a clear,
general overview of the
subject, and gives key
information that you need
to know about it.

CAPTIONS AND
ANNOTATIONS
Each illustration has a
caption. Annotations, in
italics, point out features of
an illustration.

RUNNING HEADS
These remind you which section you are in. The top of the left-hand page gives the section name. The right-hand page gives the subject. This page comes from the section on light horses.

FACT BOXES
Many pages have fact boxes. These contain at-a-glance information about the horse featured on that page. This fact box gives interesting facts about the history of the Cleveland Bay.

SIZE INDICATORS
These show the average height of the horse is measured in hands. One hand is equal to 4 in (10 cm), the approximate breadth of a large hand.

16

Caption   *Running head*

CLEVELAND BAY

TRADING PLACES
The Cleveland Bay is developed from a stew of English horses, and Andalusians and Barbs brought on trading ships from Spain and North Africa to Cleveland during the 1600s. It later became known as the most powerful coach horse in Europe.

In the late 1700s, Cleveland Bays helped the development of the Bavarian Warmblood, giving it strength and stamina. This German breed is kept as a competition and carriage horse.

Tail is usually black, but grey hairs are a sign of purity.

Powerful quarters help the horse jump well.

Long legs give the horse literary height.

95

Annotation   *Fact box*

BAVARIAN WARMBLOOD

CLEVELAND BAY FACTS
• Cleveland Bays used to be called Chapmen Horses after traveling salesmen (chapmen) who used these horses to pull their carts.
• In 1962, Queen Elizabeth II bought and bred one of the last four stallions to save the breed from extinction.
• Cleveland Bays have been used in plow and draft horses on farms, as packhorses, and for carrying coal.

RECORDS AND FACTS
THE SHEER DIVERSITY of horse types and breeds found around the world has led to a number of amazing facts and figures. Although some are unusual phenomena, many are connected with the horse's association with people, a relationship that goes back over 6,000 years.

REFERENCE SECTION
The reference section pages are yellow and appear at the back of the book. On these, you will find useful facts, figures, and charts. These pages give horse records, such as the biggest and smallest, and important horse care information.

LABELS
For greater clarity, some pictures have labels. They may give extra information, or identify a picture when it is not obvious from the text what it is.

INDEX
You will find an index at the back of *Pockets: Horses*. This acts as a species and a subject index. Every subject and type of horse covered in the book are listed alphabetically.

INTRODUCTION
TO HORSES

WHAT IS A HORSE? 12
THE HORSE IN HISTORY 14
THE FIRST HORSES 18
MAIN HORSE TYPES 20
BODY AND CONFORMATION 22
COAT COLORS 26
MOVEMENT 30
FOOD AND DIET 32
BEHAVIOR 34
LIFE CYCLE OF A HORSE 36
USES OF THE HORSE 40
HORSE RIDING 44

WHAT IS A HORSE?

SOME 60 MILLION YEARS AGO the first horses ran on the plains of North America. The modern horse has single-hooved feet and a greater length of leg than its earlier ancestors. Like all mammals, horses suckle their young, and as herbivores, their natural food is grass. They are social creatures, and prefer to live in groups.

Long tail helps to keep flies off the body

Deep girth provides an adequate lung capacity

Powerful muscles supply propulsive thrust in movement

Hooves are made of a protein called keratin

HORSE FACTS

• Horses are measured from the ground up to the withers, which is the highest point of the shoulders.

• In 1910, North America had about 20 million domestic horses.

• There are over 150 officially recognized horse and pony breeds.

• Most modern horse breeds have been deliberately created to do a specific task.

Long hair on the back of the neck is called a mane

Horses have an excellent sense of hearing

Withers

Long head and neck allow horse to graze while standing

HORSES AND HUMANS
As this cave painting shows, early humans hunted horses for their meat and skin. By keeping horses in herds, these essential items became more readily available. Eventually, horses were used for riding and pulling carts, and later they were bred to perform all kinds of work.

It takes over two years for a horse foal to take on adult proportions

Long legs developed to run from danger

BORN TO RUN
Both wild and domestic horses give birth to fully developed offspring. This is because in the wild the young foal must keep up with its mother and the herd, as well as escaping from predators.

THE HORSE IN HISTORY

DOMESTICATION OF HORSES began in Asia about 5,000 to 6,000 years ago. Originally this provided tribes with meat, milk, hides, and helped to increase their mobility. Horses were later used to pull loads and then chariots. This led to horsepower becoming a vital component in transportation and warfare.

Horse

Hinny

BEFORE HORSES
Oxen or onagers were domesticated before horses. This Mesopotamian mosaic of 2500 BC shows a team of onagers pulling a chariot.

CHARIOTS
After horse-riding tribes made contact with the Egyptians, horses and hinnies (the offspring of a male horse and a female donkey) became a popular means of transportation in Egypt. Both animals are painted on this Egyptian tomb of c.1400 BC.

CONSTELLATION OF PEGASUS

MYTHOLOGICAL STORIES
According to ancient Greek mythology, Pegasus, a winged horse, rose from the severed head of the gorgon Medusa. Athena, goddess of wisdom, caught it and tamed it with a golden bridle. Later, Greek astronomers gave the name Pegasus to a group of stars in the northern sky.

HUNTING FOR PLEASURE
Horses have been used for hunting for centuries. This mosaic is from late 5th or 6th century North Africa.

6TH CENTURY PERSIAN PLATE

EMPIRE BUILDERS
In the 6th century, Persians used horses to create the first sizable empire. The Persians were excellent riders and defeated their enemies with horse-drawn chariots and cavalry. They also built roads and set up an efficient postal system, relying on horses, to help them run their domain.

More horses in history

Before the arrival of the steam engine, just about everything was moved by horses. People traveled in carts and carriages, and goods went by pack horses on roads or by horse-drawn barges on canals. In war, horses were used in cavalry formations and for the movement of guns and supplies. Horses were popular as children's toys, much in the same way as cars are today.

BARGE HORSES
The first canal barges in the 18th century were pulled by horses on a towpath beside the water. Loads of up to 50 tons (tonnes) were hauled at speeds of about 2 mph (3.3 km/h).

JOUSTING
In 15th-century Europe, mounted knights prepared for war by jousting. In this sport, a knight tried to unhorse his opponent or break his own lance against the other's shield. A fully loaded jousting horse carried around 419 lb (190 kg) of knight, armor, and saddle.

Brightly colored caparison covers horse

Leather gauntlet or glove

Heavy chain mail armor

HISTORICAL FACTS
• El Cid, the Christian warrior, called his horse *Babieca*, the Spanish word for "stupid."

• A "freelance" was a medieval mercenary with a horse and lance.

• An Austrian horse-drawn railway opened in 1852; it was 124 miles (200 km) long.

19TH CENTURY
PHAETON CARRIAGE

*Phaetons were
pulled by either one
or two horses*

CITY TRANSPORTATION
Before the early 20th century, much of the transportation in cities was horse-powered. Horses pulled cabs, buses, trams, and private carriages. The phaeton was a light, four-wheeled vehicle that was designed to be driven by its owner. It became fashionable in the 19th century.

*Metal helm, the largest and
heaviest type of helmet*

18TH-CENTURY
ROCKING
HORSE

TOYS
As the horse played such a large part in everyday life, it naturally became popular as a children's toy. Rocking horses were invented in the early 1600s.

*Wooden lance
up to 8 ft
(2.5 m) long has
blunted tip to
prevent injury*

*Saddle has a high
back to help absorb
shock of impact*

THE FIRST HORSES

THE ORIGINS OF today's horses can
be traced back over 60 million
years. The first horses probably
started to evolve in what is now
the southeastern part of North
America, before the continents
split and moved to their present
positions. Horses became extinct
there about 8,000 years ago, but
thrived in Asia, Africa, and Europe.

HIPPARION
This was the last of the
three-toed horses. Its
remains have been found
in Europe, Asia, and
Africa, where it lived up
to 15,000 years ago.

SKULL
_Small teeth
ideal for
browsing_

FOUR-TOED FOOT

_Four toes on front feet
good for marshy land_

EOHIPPUS
This small browsing
animal, no bigger than a
hare, was the ancestor of
the modern horse. It
became extinct about
40 million years ago.

SKULL
_Narrow jaw
and longer head_

THREE-TOED FOOT

_Fewer toes better for
running on hard ground_

MESOHIPPUS
As the forests began to
thin out, and the land
became drier and harder,
early horses such as
Mesohippus could run and
trot over long distances.

SKULL
_Incisor
teeth begin
to develop_

THREE-TOED FOOT

_Outside toes are
still prominent_

MIOHIPPUS
This was a more advanced
form of _Mesohippus_ and
lived around 30 million
years ago. It had still to
develop the galloping
action of modern horses.

ORIGINS

Land bridges helped horses to establish their present distribution. The Bering land bridge between North America and Asia was cut at the end of the last Ice Age because of the rising sea level. This separated the populations of horses.

Bering land bridge

60 MILLION YEARS AGO

PRESENT DAY

FIRST HORSE FACTS

• Scientists suspect that a disease wiped out the early North American horses.

• The first *Eohippus* was discovered in 1867 in Wyoming.

• The wild ancestral horses of South America are all extinct.

SKULL

Heavy jaw. holds grass-chewing molar teeth

THREE-TOED FOOT

Two side toes are kept off the ground and body is supported by central toe

SKULL

Teeth fully evolved for grazing

ONE-TOED FOOT

First single hoof of today's modern breeds

MERYCHIPPUS

A long neck helped *Merychippus* graze, rather than browse. This horse lived on the prairies of present-day Nebraska, in the North American midwest, about 15 million years ago.

PLIOHIPPUS

The direct ancestor of the modern horse, *Pliohippus* lived about six million years ago. It had the general proportions of today's equines and stood around 48 in (122 cm) high at the shoulder.

19

MAIN HORSE TYPES

MOST MODERN HORSES are thought to be descended
from four types which inhabited Europe and Asia over
6,000 years ago. Their features can still be seen in
some breeds today. Domestication led to the variety of
modern breeds and their spread across the world.

*Broad
forehead with
straight profile*

*Lean with
narrow body*

PONY TYPE 1
This hardy pony looked similar to today's
Exmoor breed of Great Britain. It lived
in northwestern Europe.

HORSE TYPE 1
Originating from central Asia, this horse
lived in dry, arid conditions and
resembled the modern Akhal-Teke.

*Small
head*

PONY TYPE 2
Similar to Przewalski's horse, the Type 2
was powerfully built with a heavy head
and roamed over northern Eurasia.

HORSE TYPE 2
Living in the hot deserts of western
Asia, this slim horse was possibly the
ancestor of the Arabian and Caspian.

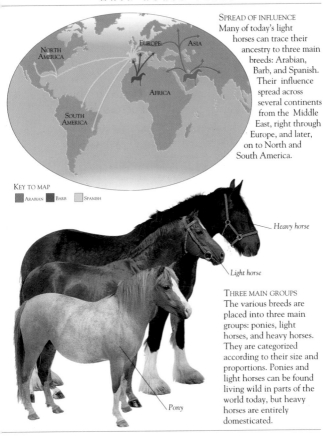

SPREAD OF INFLUENCE
Many of today's light horses can trace their ancestry to three main breeds: Arabian, Barb, and Spanish. Their influence spread across several continents from the Middle East, right through Europe, and later, on to North and South America.

KEY TO MAP
ARABIAN   BARB   SPANISH

Heavy horse

Light horse

THREE MAIN GROUPS
The various breeds are placed into three main groups: ponies, light horses, and heavy horses. They are categorized according to their size and proportions. Ponies and light horses can be found living wild in parts of the world today, but heavy horses are entirely domesticated.

Pony

BODY AND CONFORMATION

A HORSE'S BODY IS perfectly designed for its way of
life. The neck is long so it can stoop to graze, and
long, muscular legs allow it to run away from danger.
The proportions of a horse's body, or conformation,
may vary according to the
group or breed.

Points

The external features of a
horse are called the points.
Each point has a different
name and together they
make up the horse's
conformation.

Mane

Crest

Withers

Throat

Jugular groove

Shoulder

Breast

Poll

Neck

Ear

Eye

Forehead

Facial crest

Nasal bone

Knee joint

Cannon bone

Cheek

Nostril

Lower jaw

Muzzle

Fetlock joint

Upper lip

Lower lip

PROPORTION
In a perfectly proportioned horse, certain measurements of the body should all be equal. Those shown in blue should correspond to each other, as should the lines drawn in both red and gray.

Head should be same size as side of blue squares

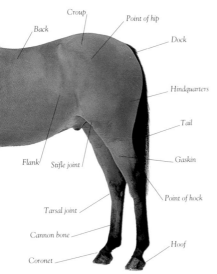

Croup

Back

Point of hip

Dock

Hindquarters

Tail

Gaskin

Flank

Stifle joint

Point of hock

Tarsal joint

Cannon bone

Hoof

Coronet

FRONT AND REAR LIMBS
When viewed from the front, a line from the shoulder should pass through the center of the knees, fetlock, and foot. A straight line should also pass through the rear legs.

ANATOMICAL FACTS

• The body and head of a horse are streamlined and this helps to reduce wind resistance.

• A long neck and well-sloped shoulders may indicate that the horse is fast and good for riding.

• Large eyes usually show not only that the horse has good vision, but also a calm nature and intelligence.

Skeleton and muscles

The framework of the horse consists of a skeleton, made up of a number of connected bones that are moved by muscles. Along the spinal, or vertebral, column, which runs from the head to the tail, is the spinal cord – the connection between the horse's brain and body. When a horse wants to move, it sends a message from its brain down the cord via nerves to signal the appropriate muscle.

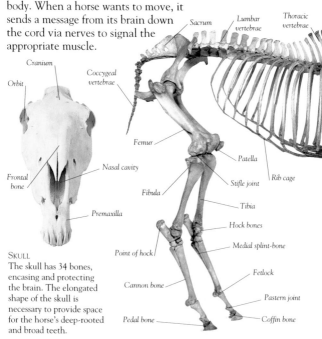

Sacrum

Lumbar vertebrae

Thoracic vertebrae

Cranium

Coccygeal vertebrae

Orbit

Femur

Patella

Rib cage

Frontal bone

Nasal cavity

Stifle joint

Fibula

Tibia

Premaxilla

Hock bones

Medial splint-bone

Point of hock

Fetlock

Cannon bone

Pastern joint

Pedal bone

Coffin bone

SKULL
The skull has 34 bones, encasing and protecting the brain. The elongated shape of the skull is necessary to provide space for the horse's deep-rooted and broad teeth.

SKELETON

The skeleton is a strong, jointed framework, made up of about 250 bones that support and protect the soft tissues of the body. The vertebrae of the spine keep the body rigid and strong.

Orbit

Cranium

Nasal bone

Atlas

Axis

Cervical vertebrae

Mandible

Scapula

Scapular spine

Shoulder joint

Sternum

Humerus

Ulna

Radius

Carpals

Suspensory ligament

Cannon bone

Fetlock joint

Pastern

Coffin joint

MUSCLES

Gluteal fascia

External intercostal

Trapezius

Splenius

Triceps

Biceps femoris

Abdominal

Pectoral

Carpal

Ligament binds bones together

Tendon attaches muscle to bone

MUSCLE FACTS

• foreleg ligaments and tendons govern movement and prevent muscle damage.

• Muscle development helps to create the horse's overall outline.

• Horses are sometimes made to swim in large water baths to help strengthen tired or injured muscles.

MUSCLES

A horse has muscles in every part of its body. These are made up of fibrous bands of tissue that relax and contract to produce movement. There are two types of muscles: voluntary muscles, which are near to thesurface and controlled by the horse, and involuntary muscles, which control the internal organs.

COAT COLORS

HORSES COME IN a variety of colors, patterns, and markings. Some breeds include horses of different colors, while others, such as the Palomino, are defined as breeds primarily by the color of their body, mane, and tail, and certain distinguishing marks.

UNIQUE PATTERN
The zebra's striped pattern consists of black stripes on a white coat.

GRAY
White and black hairs, over black skin.

FLEABITTEN
Gray coat, flecked with brown specks of hair.

DAPPLE GRAY
Gray base, with rings made of dark gray hairs.

PALOMINO
Gold, with white mane and tail; little black.

CHESTNUT
Golden, varying from pale to rich reddish gold.

LIVER CHESTNUT
Darkest possible shade of chestnut coloring.

BAY
Reddish brown to dark gold, with black points.

BROWN
Black and brown, with black mane, tail, and legs.

BLACK
Solid black, sometimes with small white marks.

STRAWBERRY-ROAN
Chestnut body color, mixed with white hairs.

BLUE ROAN
Black or brown coat hairs mixed with some white.

DUN
Either yellow, blue, or mousebrown color.

SPOTTED
Small spots; sometimes termed Appaloosa color.

SKEWBALD
Base color broken by large patches of white.

PIEBALD
Black and white patches in no fixed pattern.

Patterns and markings

Individual horses can be identified by body markings, which can be either natural or acquired. Natural markings are often areas of white hair on the head, legs, and hooves. Acquired markings are the result of branding or injury. Branding has been done for more than 2,000 years and can help to identify the horse if it is stolen.

FACE MARKINGS
While some breeds are defined by their coat patterns, face markings help to identify individual horses. The most common face markings are named below.

BLAZE

WHITE MUZZLE   SNIP   LIP MARKS   WHITE FACE

STRIPE   STAR AND STRIPE   STAR

ERMINE   SOCK   STOCKING   ZEBRA

LEG MARKINGS
These markings are often white. They are called ermine
if they are just above the hoof, a sock if they extend
below the knee, and a stocking when extending
above the knee. Zebra markings are dark rings.

HOOF MARKINGS
The blue hoof is
made of hard blue
horn and is most
often associated
with ponies.
Hooves of black
and white
vertical stripes
are seen on the
Appaloosa and
other spotted
horse breeds.

BLUE HOOF   STRIPED HOOF

DORSAL STRIPE
This mark extends from the
tail to the withers. It is found
on primitive horses such as
the Tarpan, and is associated
with dun-colored coats.

IDENTITY MARKINGS
Artificial markings help identify
ownership and sometimes breed.
Brand marks are applied by a hot
iron rod which stops the hair
from growing back. Freeze marks
are frozen on in a similar way.

BRAND MARK   FREEZE MARK

MOVEMENT

HORSES HAVE FOUR TYPES of movement, called paces.
These are the walk, trot, canter, and gallop. The walk
is the slowest pace. The horse can then accelerate to
a trot, going faster still when cantering. Running at
top speed is galloping. In every case, the hooves touch
down in a different sequence called a gait.

ACTION
The word describes the movement
of the skeletal frame in
locomotion. The sequence
of footfalls is different
for each gait; the walk
is a four-beat gait,
trot is two, and
canter three.

*Slope of shoulders
directly influences
movement*

*A horse walks at about
3–5 mph (8 km/h)
and can gallop for
short distances up to
40 mph (60 km/h)*

WALKING
When a horse walks, it places its four
legs on the ground in regular suc-
cession. The strides are of equal distance and their length depends on the
size of the horse and its conformation.

*On left-handed turns a
horse "leads" at canter
and gallop with the left
foreleg and vice versa*

JUMPING
The horse uses its
hindlegs to power its
leap forward and upward.
As it jumps, it folds
its legs under its body,
then stretches down,
touching the ground
with one foreleg, immediately
followed by the other.

*Legs are folded
under body to
avoid obstacles*

*Horses will
instinctively jump
obstructions*

HARDY BREED
The Criollo from Argentina is
often regarded as the most
robust breed in the world.
Descended from Spanish stock,
it is tough and capable of
great endurance.

*A foal can keep up
with its mother within
hours of its birth*

MOVEMENT FACTS

• Ponies lift their feet
and have a higher
knee action, being
adapted to life on
much rougher terrain.

• Light horses hardly
bend their knees. This
allows each stride to
cover more ground.

• A straighter angle in
the shoulder of a heavy
horse gives shorter,
elevated strides with
more pulling power.

FOOD AND DIET

LIKE ANY ANIMAL, horses get their energy from food. They are herbivores, which means they do not eat meat. In the wild, horses can survive on grass and herbs as long as their grazing area is large enough. In the winter, when it is cold and there is less food, wild horses get out of condition, while in the summer they put on weight.

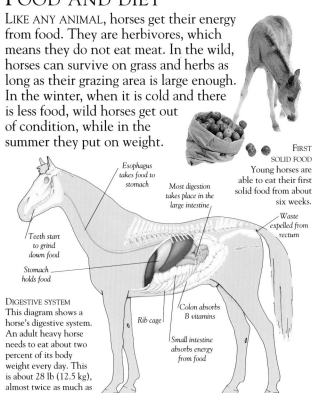

FIRST
SOLID FOOD
Young horses are able to eat their first solid food from about six weeks.

Esophagus takes food to stomach

Most digestion takes place in the large intestine

Waste expelled from rectum

Teeth start to grind down food

Stomach holds food

DIGESTIVE SYSTEM
This diagram shows a horse's digestive system. An adult heavy horse needs to eat about two percent of its body weight every day. This is about 28 lb (12.5 kg), almost twice as much as a pony eats per day.

Rib cage

Colon absorbs B vitamins

Small intestine absorbs energy from food

TEETH AND JAWS

Grazing wears down the foal's milk teeth and by the time the horse is five, these are replaced by a set of 40 adult teeth. The incisors cut the food into small pieces and the molars grind it down, ready for digestion.

Hinge with top jaw

Mandible

Eye socket

Hard palate

Molars

Bottom incisors

Canines

Top incisors

BOTTOM JAW   TOP JAW

FOOD DANGERS

• Plants like deadly nightshade, bracken, and ragwort may poison a horse if it eats even a small quantity. Pastures where horses are left to graze must be cleared of these plants.

• Horses should not graze in an area within 14 days of any spraying.

BALANCED DIET

Horses need a balanced diet, with enough vitamins and minerals to help them stay healthy and in condition. Horses should be fed little and often. Water with the meal keeps the horse from becoming dehydrated.

Fruit and root vegetables must be chopped up lengthwise so the horse does not choke.

Feed bowl holds carrots, corn, linseed, nuts, chaff, and a slice of apple

Hay is grass that has been cut and dried.

Bucket of clean, fresh water

BEHAVIOR

TODAY'S DOMESTIC HORSES show the same patterns of behavior as their wild ancestors. The herd instinct still dominates, and horses prefer to be kept in groups rather than on their own. Much of their behavior is linked to the way they communicate with other horses.

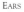

Horses sleep for only short periods at a time.

SLEEPING

Horses are able to sleep standing up. In the wild, this increases their chances of escaping from predators.

EARS

The position of a horse's ears is an important indicator of its mood. If the ears point forward, this shows curiosity. When the horse is uncertain, it keeps one ear forward and the other backward.

SHIRE HORSE

FLEHMENING

When a mare is close to a stallion, the stallion may fold back his lips and draw air into his mouth to detect the mare's scent to sense if she is ready to mate. This action is called flehmening.

MUTUAL GROOMING

Horses indulge in mutual grooming as a sign of a close relationship. They will gently nuzzle each other's backs, nibbling at the hair. Such sessions may last for several minutes at a time.

REARING
A stallion rears
up to intimidate
a rival, often
lashing out
with his front
feet at the
same time.

*Horse uses its
front legs to
balance*

*Horses
often rear
in play.*

ROLLING OVER
By rolling, a horse can exercise the
muscles in its back, and also clean its
coat. Horses often roll when turned
out to graze in
a field.

*Stallions rear
naturally
in the wild.*

*Horses nuzzle
each other to
establish their
relationship.*

SHETLAND
PONY

BEHAVIORAL FACTS
• Horses will call out
to warn others of
approaching danger.
• The tail is used as a
fly swish rather than
for communication.
• Repeated pawing at
the ground with the
hooves is often a sign
of nervousness.
• A horse's ears are
very mobile and can
rotate independently
in a full circle.

LIFE CYCLE OF A HORSE

MARES NEED ONLY BE three or four years old before they are ready to give birth. After mating, it is almost a year before the foal is born and it takes another five before it becomes a fully grown adult horse. Most horses have a life span of around 25 years.

Early development

A mare is ready to mate at intervals of roughly three weeks from spring to autumn. During these intervals, which last five to seven days, she is said to be in heat and will be ready to accept an approach by a stallion.

MATING
When a mare is in heat, her behavior changes and she often seeks the company of other horses more than is usual.

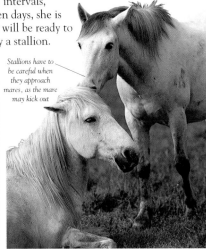

Stallions have to be careful when they approach mares, as the mare may kick out

DEVELOPMENT FACTS

• Male foals usually spend more time in the womb than females.

• It is not obvious that a mare is pregnant until after five months.

• The mare's belly drops before she is ready to give birth.

• Mares can give birth at two years old, but this is unusual.

• It is rare for a horse to give birth to twins.

Foal's gender is
already established

2 MONTHS

Foal positions itself
to be born head first

11 MONTHS

EMBRYO DEVELOPMENT
Pregnancy usually lasts 11
months. The development
of the foal occurs during
the early part, with the
growth phase taking
place toward the end.
At birth, a foal will be
at least 43 in (109 cm)
long, and weigh up to
107 lb (49 kg).

Hooves are formed
and hair grows
around the lips

4 MONTHS

Dramatic
increase in
weight occurs

10 MONTHS

Hair covers most of
the body and foal
is about 22 in
(56 cm) long

6 MONTHS

Mane starts
to develop and
foal weighs up to
42 lb (19 kg)

8 MONTHS

Growing up

The usual time for a foal to be born is during early summer, when grass and other food is most plentiful, to help the mare's milk supply. Horses develop quickly from young foals into adults. A horse can be independent of its mother by the time it is six months old reaching full adult size between the ages of four and five years. It is at its strongest between the ages of five and 15.

Mare licks foal clean.

Foals take milk at frequent intervals.

1 NEWBORN
A new foal can stand on its feet within half an hour of its birth. It is carefully watched over by its mother.

Large eyes

Legs are long in proportion to the body

2 TWO WEEKS
After two weeks, the foal is used to walking. To give it extra stability, it stands with its rear legs slightly apart, as it cannot yet straighten its legs. The hooves are small and soft. The tail is short and bushy, while the mane stands up on its neck and is light and feathery.

3 FIVE WEEKS
At five weeks, the foal still has a soft woolly coat, known as milk hair. The upper bones of its legs become longer, and the foal can now stand upright.

4 EIGHT WEEKS
The foal lives solely on its mother's milk for its first two months, after which it gradually begins to eat grass, until it is fully weaned at around six months old. After two months, the foal's fluffy milk hair begins to be shed and is replaced by its adult coat.

Hindquarters become noticeably more muscular

Digestion changes during weaning

Muscles become firmer

5 FOUR MONTHS
The foal's body has grown to adult proportions. The neck and tail have lengthened, and the legs continue to become stronger as their muscles develop further. The hooves also become harder.

GROWING-UP FACTS

• As soon as they are born, new foals shiver to maintain their body temperature.

• The mother's first milk, called colostrum, contains antibodies, which protect the foal against infections.

• After weaning, horse breeders usually give foals a concentrated feed with supplements to ensure that the foals grow healthy.

USES OF THE HORSE

IN SPITE OF THE SPREAD of mechanization, the horse
still has a place in society. Today, horses can be found
at work in cities, forests, and farmland. While
traditional horse sports, like racing and steeple-chasing,
remain popular, they are now being joined
by leisure activities such as trail riding.

Working horses

Horses work in forests because they cause less
damage than tractors. Farmers in developing
countries also find horses easy to keep, as they
can live off the land. Though no longer used in
war, horses are retained in many countries for
ceremonial duties and the police horse
has so far proved irreplaceable.

London police
horses undergo
about 40 weeks
of training.

MULE TRAINS
Even in the late 20th century, it has
been hard to find anything to replace
the mule to transport goods over
uneven ground. Mules are still used in
India, China, and Southeast Asia.

ROYAL
ARTILLERY
HORSE AND
RIDER

CEREMONIAL DUTIES
Many countries still use horses for ceremonial duties. This dates from wars where horses were used as cavalry and to haul artillery.

WORKING HORSE FACTS
• More horses are bred in the United States for leisure riding than for herding cattle.

• India employs more mounted police than any other country in the world.

• Heavy horses are used in Canadian forests to pull up trees and take them away and to cultivate the soil afterward.

POLICE HORSES
Mounted police can be seen in many cities today. Horses offer the rider a good view and mobility, and can move through crowds more easily than either motorcycles or cars.

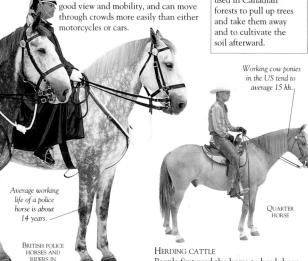

Working cow ponies in the US tend to average 15 hh.

Average working life of a police horse is about 14 years.

QUARTER
HORSE

BRITISH POLICE
HORSES AND
RIDERS IN
CEREMONIAL
DRESS

HERDING CATTLE
People first used the horse to herd sheep and cattle over 6,000 years ago and still do so in North America and Australia.

Horses for sport and leisure

Since the end of World War II, there has been a tremendous increase in the use of the horse for pleasure. Sports such as horse racing remain as popular as ever, and interest in such competition as show jumping and dressage has been heightened by television. Riding holidays are now a popular and relaxing pastime for many people.

POLO
Originating in Persia, polo was played at least 2,500 years ago by teams of up to 1,000 players. Today, two teams of four try to knock a ball into a goal with a long mallet.

DRESSAGE
A dressage test lasts about 5 minutes and shows the rider's control and the training of the horse. The sport has wide appeal and competitions are held at every level.

Rider's actions are well controlled

A hard hat protects the rider's head in case of a fall.

Rider sits on the horse's center of balance.

Pony will cover 3–4 miles (4.8–6.4 km) in an hour

More experienced horse and rider leads trail ride.

RACEHORSES
Horse racing has become a huge international industry. This statue in the Kentucky Horse Park, US, is of the famous racehorse Man O' War, or Big Red, who was beaten only once in 21 races. When he died in 1947, more than 1,000 people attended his funeral.

HORSE SPORTS FACTS
• The longest-running horse race is the Palio in Siena, Italy, begun in the 1200s and still run today. The winning horse attends a special banquet afterward.

• The word polo comes from the Tibetan *pulu*, meaning ball.

• The first steeplechase was held in 1830 at St. Albans, England.

Riders learn to use aids such as the reins.

Each rider keeps a pony-length away from the next.

A novice rider is given a well-trained horse.

Many ponies are bred specifically for riding schools.

RIDING HOLIDAYS
Those who want to ride occasionally or just for pleasure, can take a riding holiday. These rides can last a single day or a whole week and demand little skill. The distance covered in each day varies between 25–50 miles (40–80 km). Trips are often supervised and provide an opportunity to reach beautiful and inaccessible areas of a country.

HORSEBACK RIDING

PEOPLE HAVE RIDDEN HORSES for many different reasons. Even before the invention of the wheel, horses provided fast transportation. Soldiers rode horses during wartime and explorers often traveled on horseback over unknown territory.

Riding styles

One of the oldest schools of riding is that of the Iberian Peninsula in Portugal and Spain. The techniques and swift movements originate with cattle herding and the practice of mounted bullfighting.

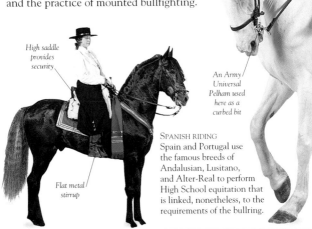

High saddle provides security

An Army Universal Pelham used here as a curbed bit

Flat metal stirrup

SPANISH RIDING
Spain and Portugal use the famous breeds of Andalusian, Lusitano, and Alter-Real to perform High School equitation that is linked, nonetheless, to the requirements of the bullring.

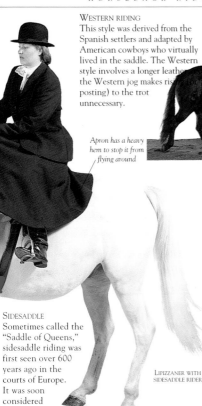

WESTERN RIDING
This style was derived from the
Spanish settlers and adapted by
American cowboys who virtually
lived in the saddle. The Western
style involves a longer leather
the Western jog makes risi
posting) to the trot
unnecessary.

*The Western horse
can be trained in a
bitless Hackamore
bridle*

*Apron has a heavy
hem to stop it from
flying around*

CLASSICAL RIDING SCHOOL
Riding as a trained skill
was first made popular in
Italy in the 16th century.

SIDESADDLE
Sometimes called the
"Saddle of Queens,"
sidesaddle riding was
first seen over 600
years ago in the
courts of Europe.
It was soon
considered
unladylike
to ride astride.

LIPIZZANER WITH
SIDESADDLE RIDER

RIDING STYLE FACTS
• Classical riding of the
Renaissance was based
on the Spanish horse of
the period.
• Women rode astride
until the 15th century.
• In classical riding,
the horse's leaps or
kicks are called "airs."

Equipment

In the early days, horses were ridden either bareback or with a simple cloth pad and were guided by a rope attached to their lower jaw. It was only during the late Roman period that saddles were used for the first time. Stirrups were probably introduced to Europe by the Huns under Attila in the 5th century.

BIT
This long-cheeked curb bit dates from the 16th century. It has a shaped mouthpiece that allows room for the horse's tongue.

Rowel pricks the horse's side

BRASS ROWEL SPUR FROM SOUTH AMERICA, c.1800

Buckle attaches spur to boot

MOTIVATION
Spurs are used to urge a horse to go forward. In the past, some particularly cruel spurs were devised which cut into the horse's side, but today they never have sharp edges.

Chinese slipper stirrup, 11th century

LEG AID
Stirrups support the rider, enabling long distances to be covered comfortably. When riding at speed, a shorter stirrup leather is used, as in the case of race riding.

SADDLE
This is the type of saddle used in the classical schools of the 18th century. It was called *Selle à Piquer*.

MODERN TACK

Horse equipment is called tack. Advances in manufacturing techniques and materials have helped improve the range of equipment now available.

Browband

Bridle Cheekpiece

Numnah

Shaped saddle

Hard hat with silk covering

Flash noseband

Leather reins

Jodhpurs are specially cut for comfort

Stirrups are run up to keep them out of the way

A girth holds the saddle in position

Rubber or leather boots

EQUIPMENT FACTS

• Metal bits were first introduced between 13,000 and 12,000 BC.

• Medieval saddles had high backs for knights to brace themselves against in battle.

• The 5th century Huns were among the first to use stirrups.

PONIES

INTRODUCTION TO PONIES 50

SHETLAND 52

HIGHLAND 54

FELL AND DALES 56

EXMOOR AND DARTMOOR 58

NEW FOREST PONY 60

WELSH MOUNTAIN PONY
AND AUSTRALIAN PONY 62

CONNEMARA 64

CHINCOTEAGUE 66

HAFLINGER 68

CASPIAN 70

FALABELLA 72

ICELANDIC HORSE 74

INTRODUCTION TO PONIES

PONIES HAVE BEEN AROUND ever since the equine species evolved. They belong, of course, to the genus *Equus* but are distinguished by particular characteristics from today's breeds. Ponies are smaller, no taller than 14.2 hands high, with shorter legs in relation to their height. They also live longer and are hardier.

WARRIOR BREED
Despite their small size, ponies were used as war horses by European warriors such as Vikings.

PONY POWER
In the past, ponies provided a means of transportation. Stronger for their size than horses, ponies were able to pull traps (small carts) without difficulty. Ponies are now popular for use in driving competitions.

Thick tail keeps out the cold

Wooden spoked wheels

19TH-CENTURY
LIVERPOOL
PONY GIG

Strong hind-
quarters

Head is
similar to a
Thoroughbred's

Limbs and joints
must be strong
and well-formed

POLO PONY
This is not a breed, but a type of pony
produced for a particular purpose. Polo
demands that the animal must be fast and surefooted. So, the first polo ponies were bred by
crossing Thoroughbreds for speed, and ponies
for stability.

PONY FACTS
• The word pony
comes from the French
word *poulenet*, which is
a foal or young horse.
• Ponies were first used
down coal mines in the
1600s, hauling wagons
of coal from the pit
face to the surface.
• Robert the Bruce of
Scotland defeated an
English army in 1314,
using light cavalry
mounted on ponies.

Short, powerful
limbs with
strong bones

Hard feet,
notably free
from disease

HARD HOOF
Ponies are more surefooted than
horses. They have particularly
tough hooves and seldom go lame.
These characteristics are derived
from their former mountain and
moorland environment.

SHETLAND

THESE PONIES WERE named after the bleak Shetland
Islands off the northeast coast of Scotland, where
they have been bred for more than 2,000 years. Their
ancestors were either brought over from the mainland
or from Scandinavia. In spite of their small size, the
Shetlands are a tough
and hardy breed.

Weather-resistant
coat, double-layered
in winter

LARGE AND SMALL
As more people have kept
Shetlands, some breeders
have developed a smaller
pony for use as a pet.
This has given rise to the
Miniature Shetland which
has proved popular.

Muscular neck

NATIVE HABITAT
There are no trees on the Shetland Islands to
provide firewood, so islanders dug up peat on the
moors for fuel. This was carried to their villages by
the ponies, which are
very strong for
their small size.

Strong,
rounded
feet

10

THELWELL CARTOON
The Shetland is a good choice for a young rider, but it can get fat if not exercised regularly – as this drawing by the British cartoonist Thelwell shows.

AMERICAN SHETLAND
This modern breed is the result of combining the Shetland primarily with Hackney blood, and bears no close resemblance to its island ancestor. The American pony is slimmer and has a more refined look.

Hair of mane and tail is thin and usually soft

RIDING PONY
Although the Shetland is probably more suited to harness, it can be used as a first riding pony for small children. It is very surefooted and thrives on a minimum feed ration.

Long-haired tail, especially full to protect against the weather

Back legs are strong and firm

HIGHLAND

THE LARGEST AND STRONGEST of Britain's ponies is the Highland. Originally small, the size and strength of these ponies was increased by crossings with Percheron heavy horses in the 16th century. Later, Arab input made them more suitable for riding. Today's Highland combines strength with an easygoing nature.

Wide forehead combined with short head

Neck is strong and arched

Broad, wide nostrils

Strong forelegs with large, flat knees

Long hair is soft and silky

CAVE PAINTINGS
This painting from cave walls at Lascaux, France, dates back about 14,000 years to the end of the last Ice Age. Some of these drawings bear a striking resemblance to the modern dun-colored Highland.

Pony reckoned to be about 13 hh

Western Isles

SCOTLAND

IRELAND

ENGLAND

HIGHLAND HOMELAND
Ponies have lived in the upland areas of northern Scotland and on some of the nearby Western Isles for more than 10,000 years. They are still used in the forest, for trekking, and in harness.

COLORED COATS
Highlands are bred in many colors. This pony is dun with a black mane and tail, and black lower legs. A dense double-layered coat gives good protection in bad weather conditions.

HIGHLAND FACTS

• In the circus ring, a Highland has carried seven adults on its back, weighing a total of 840 lb (380 kg).

• Many ponies have dark "eel" stripes running along the back and down the tail.

• Highland ponies were ridden in the Jacobite uprisings in Scotland during the 18th century.

Short, strong back

Tail set high and has fine, silky texture

Some have zebra-like markings on the lower leg

Hard hooves enable the pony to thrive on rough ground

14

CLYDESDALE INFLUENCE

During the 19th century, the Highland was made bigger and stronger as a result of crossings with the Clydesdale. But the breed's coarser looks were considered to be unattractive.

Longer legs than most heavy breeds

FELL AND DALES

THESE TWO MOORLAND BREEDS descend from a common root. Their early ancestor was the Friesian horse employed by Roman mercenaries guarding Hadrian's Wall (in what is now northern England). Their greatest influence however, is the swift Scottish Galloway of the 17th and 18th centuries. Both breeds are used extensively in harness for trekking.

Long tail trails close to the ground

Massive hind legs provide propulsion

14

TOUGH UPBRINGING

The natural habitat of the Fell and Dales is the rugged, hilly Pennine region of northern England. The Fell developed on the west side and the Dales on the east. The rough countryside has made both ponies hardy breeds, with plenty of stamina. They have hard feet, which do not wear down even when walking long distances over rough tracks. The ponies trot quickly and move freely.

FELL
The Fell is smaller and lighter than the Dales and was once preferred for riding. However, it could also carry heavy loads of 224 lb (102 kg) or more. It was not unusual for a pony to cover 240 miles (384 km) a week.

HACKNEY PONY
As a result of a bloodline developed in the 1880s, which was later crossbred with Trotters and Roadsters, the Fell has added to the ancestry of the Hackney Pony.

The Hackney is the supreme harness horse

DALES
In the past, the heavier-built Dales were valued as pack ponies. They carried lead ore mined on the moors to the ports of northeastern England.

Broad, open nostrils

Strong hindquarters

Broad, sloping shoulders

Tough blue horn hooves, with hair at the heels

14.2

Deep girth, with long and rounded ribs

EXMOOR AND DARTMOOR

NAMED AFTER THEIR moorland
habitats, both these ponies come
from southwestern England. The
Exmoor is the oldest British breed
of pony and its ancestors may have
roamed over Exmoor before the
Bronze Age, about 4,000 years ago.
The younger Dartmoor dates back
1000 years, but today's pony looks
little like it
did then.

WORKING PONY
Like most ponies, the
Exmoor and Dartmoor
have been used as pack
animals. The Dartmoor
used to carry tin from
mines on the moor to
nearby towns.

*Mottled coloring
on muzzle and
around the eyes*

EXMOOR PONY
These ponies have had
to adapt to survive hrsh
Exmoor winters. A fan-
like area of hair at the
top of their tail prevents
water from penetrating
and then freezing. Long
nasal passages allow cold
air to be warmed as
it is inhaled.

*Compact body
with long ribs
and deep chest*

*Thick, springy
coat provides
warmth in winter*

*Short legs and
neat hooves*

12

58

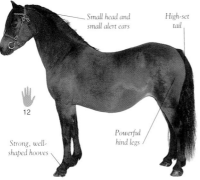

Small head and small alert ears

High-set tail

12

Powerful hind legs

Strong, well-shaped hooves

EXMOOR PONY FACTS

• The eyes of the Exmoor pony are called "toad eyes", and are hooded to protect them from the rain and snow.

• The ponies dislike dogs, possibly because of an ancestral fear of wolves which used to live on Exmoor.

• Purebred Exmoors are marked with a star-shaped brand on their left shoulder, with their herd number beneath.

DARTMOOR PONY
As a result of crossings with other breeds, the modern Dartmoor is a particularly elegant-looking pony. It does not lift its knees as high as other ponies, and has a better riding action as a result.

HARSH HABITAT
Dartmoor, in the English county of Devon, is crossed by the Dart, Tavy, and Taw rivers. Conditions here can be tough, and the ponies had to be hardy and surefooted to thrive. Today, few of these ponies are still to be seen on the moors.

NEW FOREST PONY

FOR MORE THAN a thousand years, these hardy little ponies have roamed the New Forest in southern England. Oddly, the "forest" is mainly a large expanse of moorland covered with heather. Ponies have only been allowed to stay in this area throughout the year since 1877. Until then, it was thought that there was not enough food for them. Even today, the herd is limited to 2,500 to prevent overgrazing.

Large head reflects the influence of other horse breeds.

NEW FOREST FACTS

• The New Forest Pony is the second largest of the British Mountain and Moorland ponies.

• The ponies feed on prickly shrubs in winter. In spring, they must be watched closely to stop them wandering into boggy ground, where the first shoots of grass appear.

• Speeding vehicles injure or kill about 150 ponies every year.

NEW FOREST GUARDIANS

The ponies are owned by Commoners – people who have the right to graze their stock inside the forest. Four wardens, called Agisters, organize a roundup of the animals in late summer to check for any health problems and deal with any emergencies.

PONY AUCTION
Each year some of the ponies are sold by auction. Their friendly nature means they are in great demand for young riders and for driving.

Can be any color except pinto or albino.

Straight, powerful legs and hard, round hooves

IMPROVING THE BREED
The New Forest Ponies have been purebred for only 50 years. Many breeds have played a part in their history. Once, an Arabian stallion called Zorah, owned by Queen Victoria, was released into the forest in an attempt to breed with the ponies and improve their appearance.

13

WELSH MOUNTAIN PONY AND AUSTRALIAN PONY

PONIES CAN BE related to each other, even if they live on opposite sides of the world. The Welsh Mountain Pony is the smallest and oldest of four Welsh breeds. In the early 19th century, many Welsh ponies were exported to Australia, where they played an important part in the development of the Australian Pony.

Large eyes

Wide nostrils

WELSH MOUNTAIN PONY
In the 18th century, the breed was influenced by a Thoroughbred called Merlin. In Wales, a pony is still called a "merlin".

PONIES OF THE VALLEY
Welsh Mountain Ponies still roam the Welsh valleys in some numbers.

Short, stocky body with a deep chest

Hooves are made of blue horn, which is sound and hard

12

AUSTRALIAN PONY

This breed still has a strong resemblance to its Welsh relative and can be any solid color. It is highly valued as a riding pony in Australia, where horse sports are very popular.

Neat head with long, crested neck shows Arab influence

A distinct type was established by the late 1920s

12–14

Sloping shoulders give the ponies a long stride and smooth action

VARIED MIXTURE

The early settlers of Australia brought a variety of breeds with them and the Australian Pony was developed from these.

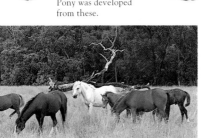

WELSH PONY FACTS

• Welsh Mountain Ponies have many attractive features, including small, pointed ears, and large, luminous eyes.

• The earliest records of these ponies date back to Roman times.

• Most of the ponies are gray, but some are bay, chestnut, or palomino.

• The ponies can survive on the sparse, reedy moorland grasses.

CONNEMARA

THE ONLY NATIVE Irish pony is the
Connemara. Its ancestors probably
resembled the ponies of Shetland,
Iceland, and Norway, but in the
16th century Galway merchants
introduced Spanish and Barb
horses into Ireland. These
interbred to produce the Irish
Hobby, forerunner of the
Connemara. The modern
Connemara is an all-round
performance pony.

CONNEMARA COUNTRY
The pony is named after
the area of Connemara,
which is part of County
Galway, on the north-
western coast of Ireland.

CONNEMARA FACTS

• Connemaras are
long-lived, very strong
and hardy, and notably
free from disease.

• The first registered
Connemara stallion,
Cannon Ball, won the
annual farmers' race at
Oughterard, Ireland, for
16 successive years.

• In Galway, this pony
was used on farms and
as a pack animal to
carry seaweed, potatoes,
peat, and corn.

Long tail is
set high

Length from
hips to the hocks
helps provide
thrust when
jumping

Gray is a com-
mon color, but
there are also the
traditional duns
as well as bays
and browns

Well-made
hind leg and
strong
firm joints

FOOD AND SIZE

On the boggy ground of their Irish homeland, Connemaras exist on a diet of sparse grass. They usually grow to a larger size when given richer food. Connemaras are often crossed with Thoroughbreds to produce competition horses.

WELSH COB INFLUENCE

In the 19th century, many Irish farmers were very poor and as a result, the Connemaras also suffered. Welsh Cobs from Britain were introduced to improve the stock.

Small, neat head shows Arab influence

HOMELAND HABITAT

The native environment of the Connemara is a wild, isolated expanse of marshes, lakes, and mountains. The ponies have been working on farms in this area for centuries.

Long neck and sloping shoulders show the pony is good for riding

14

CHINCOTEAGUE

A BOOK AND A FILM have made this delightful little pony part of the childhood of many Americans. The Chincoteague lives on two islands off the eastern coast of the US. It is said to be descended from horses that survived a shipwreck close to the coast and swam ashore.

Large head compared to the rest of the body

Heavy shoulders and straight forelimbs

HORSELIKE PONY
It is likely that Spanish blood was originally involved in the ancestry of the Chincoteague, but poor grazing and possibly inbreeding have resulted in a reduction in its size. As a result, it resembles a small horse rather than a pony.

Cannons are long and joints often poorly developed

12

Condition of the feet may vary

ISLAND HOME
The current population of around 200 Chincoteagues lives mostly on the island of Assateague, now a national park. The ponies are rounded up at the end of July for the annual sale, and made to swim across the channel to Chincoteague. Any ponies that are not sold return by the same route the following day.

CHINCOTEAGUE FACTS

• The Native American meaning of Chincoteague is "beautiful land across the waters."

• The existence of the ponies became generally known only in the 1920s.

• The ponies were made famous by the 1947 children's book entitled *Misty of Chincoteague* and a film made in 1961.

CHINCOTEAGUE ISLANDS
Both Chincoteague and Assateague islands lie off the eastern coast of the state of Virginia. Assateague was formed by a violent storm in 1933, which separated it from the mainland.

Chestnut coat

Thick coat provides good protection during the winter

COLOR VARIATIONS
Chincoteagues come in a variety of coat colors including pinto. It is claimed that they make good children's ponies if properly handled.

HAFLINGER

THIS AUSTRIAN pony originates from the village of Hafling in the Etschlander Mountains. It is descended from other local ponies, the Arabian, and extinct Alpine Heavy Horse breeds. A true Haflinger is either palomino or chestnut in color, with a flaxen mane and tail. It may be harnessed or ridden.

Flowing flaxen tail is thick and full.

Noriker's ancestors were bred by the Romans.

Broad and compact body with a deep girth

HAFLINGER FACTS

• The young foals are brought up on the Alpine fields, where their lungs develop in the thin air.

• In Austria, Haflingers are not worked until they are four years old.

• They may live for more than 40 years.

NORIKER

Half of all horses in Austria are Norikers. The ancestors of this native Austrian breed were bred by the Romans for draft and pack work. Today, it is still a working horse and can be seen near the central Alpine region, adjacent to the Austrian Tyrol, home of the Haflinger.

FLOWER BRAND
The Haflinger is also
called the Edelweiss
Pony because its brand
is the shape of
Austria's national
flower.

EDELWEISS BRAND

*Striking mane and
small, elegant head
reflect Arabian blood.*

*Large
eyes*

Big nostrils

13

HAFLINGER
This pony is powerfully
built, with well-made legs
and sloping shoulders. The
long back reflects its use as a
packpony. The ponies are
surefooted with a long stride,
even when walking across
steep mountainous terrain.

IN THE MOUNTAINS
In its native Austria,
Haflingers are harnessed to
sleighs as a means of
transportation in thick snow.
Many are kept for use in the
tourist season, when they
pull old-fashioned carriages.

CASPIAN

THOUGHT TO HAVE BEEN EXTINCT for more than a thousand years, the Caspian was rediscovered in Iran in 1965. A small herd was established at Nourouzabad by Mrs. Louise L. Firouz. Caspian societies and studs now exist in North and South America, UK and Australia.

A Caspian has one more molar than other horses

CASPIAN FACTS

• The ancient Greeks found feral horses on the edge of the Caspian Sea 2500 years ago.

• Twenty Caspians found in 1970 were used to start the Nourouzabad stud near Teheran, Iran.

• Apart from the Asiatic wild horse, the Caspian is the oldest surviving breed.

MINIATURE HORSE
The Caspian is usually described as a miniature horse rather than a pony. It has a short head, covered with the fine, thin skin of desert breeds, and large eyes and nostrils. The ears are very short and should not exceed 4.5 in (11 cm).

Shoulders slope like a horse's, giving a longer stride than true ponies

11

Strong, oval-shaped feet never need shoeing

AREA OF DISCOVERY
The pony is named after
the Caspian Sea, on the
border of Iran.

MOUNTAIN HOME
Caspians live in a remote part of Iran where there is
little rain and the temperature can vary widely. The
area is cut off from the rest of the country by the
Elburz mountains. This meant that the ponies did
not mix with other breeds and remained pure.

EGYPTIAN
CARVING

Tail is
carried
high,
as on the
Arab

CASPIAN ANCESTOR
The ancestor of the Caspian is thought to be the
smallest of the four main types of horses from which
all the main horse breeds developed. This type,
simply called Horse Type 4, lived in western Asia
and was probably no more than 9 hh. Miniature
horses similar to the Caspian have been found on
Eygptian artifacts 3,500 years old.

FALABELLA

THE SMALLEST BREED of horse in the world, the
Falabella is named after the Argentine family who
developed it. Although its size suggests it is a pony, its
proportions make it closer to a small horse. The
Falabella is generally kept as a pet, being unsuitable
for all but the very youngest rider. These little horses
may also be seen in the show ring, often
pulling scaled-down carts.

*Long, flowing,
and luxurious tail*

*Long, silky
coat*

*Head is large in
proportion to
the body*

*Straight
shoulders*

*Appaloosa
coloring*

A POPULAR PET
The friendly nature of the
Falabella has meant that it is
kept the whole world over,
especially in North America.
However, little or no
practical use can be made
of the breed and most are
kept as unusual pets.

7

SPECIAL SIZE

The size of the Falabella was achieved by intense inbreeding of the smallest specimen, a practise that can result in serious genetic weaknesses. However, now that the breed is well established, breeders try to mate unrelated Falabellas when breeding.

Legs may be weak and cow hocks are often in evidence

FALABELLA FACTS

• Miniature horses were first recorded in ancient China from 206 BC.

• Newborn Falabellas are tiny, standing about 5 hh, and weighing around 15 lb (7 kg).

• The smallest example bred by Julio Falabella was a mare barely 4 hh and weighing just over 26 lb (12 kg).

• Falabellas can pull 20 times their own weight.

COLORS AND PATTERNS

Color can be a factor contributing to the value of the Falabella. Today, there is a wide range of colors, and both solid and part colors are acceptable. Above all, the spotted Appaloosa pattern is particularly popular.

SOUTH AMERICA

Buenos Aires

PLACE OF DEVELOPMENT

In 1860, an Irishman called Newton attempted to perfect the shape of two miniature South American horses. This was later achieved by his grandson, Julio Cesar Falabella, at the family ranch close to Buenos Aires in South America.

Bay coat

Chestnut coat

ICELANDIC HORSE

IN SPITE OF ITS SMALL SIZE, this animal is described as a horse rather than a pony. Originating from Norway, the Icelandic Horse has not been crossed with any other breed for more than 1,000 years and looks much like it did in the days of the Vikings. These historic horses are still used in Iceland for transportation, farm work, and sports.

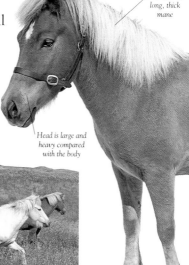

Neck carries long, thick mane

Head is large and heavy compared with the body

BARREN LANDSCAPE
The Icelandic Horse still roams across Iceland's barren landscape. It is a hardy breed, able to survive out-doors in the bitter cold of the northern winter.

GREENLAND SEA

ICELAND

ICELANDIC SETTLERS
Horses were taken to
Iceland between 935 BC
and AD 860. A hundred
years later, the Icelandic
parliament made it illegal
to import other breeds so
as to keep the Icelandic
Horse pure.

ICELANDIC FACTS
• Norsemen made
their horses fight
each other for sport.

• The Icelandic Horse
can be bred in up to
15 different colors.

• These horses have
taken part in races in
Iceland since 1874.

Chestnut coat

*Stout body and a
short, strong back
help the horse to
carry heavy loads*

NORSE SETTLERS
The ancestors of the Icelandic Horse were
brought from Norway in Norse long boats.

NORWEGIAN FJORD INFLUENCE
Together with the Tarpan, this
Scandinavian pony formed the basis of
the Icelandic Horse. It is dun in color
with a dark stripe running
from its forelock to
the tip of
its tail.

SUREFOOTED
The tough
Icelandic horse is
exceptionally
surefooted and
crosses rough
ground easily.

13–14

*Pony was
formerly
called the
Westland*

7 5

LIGHT HORSES

INTRODUCTION TO LIGHT HORSES 78

BARB 80

THOROUGHBRED 82

PINTO AND PALOMINO 84

ARABIAN 86

QUARTER HORSE 88

APPALOOSA 90

ANDALUSIAN 92

CLEVELAND BAY 94

TRAKEHNER 96

LIPIZZANER 98

AUSTRALIAN STOCK HORSE 100

MORGAN AND
DUTCH WARMBLOOD 102

INTRODUCTION TO LIGHT HORSES

THE LEAN AND athletic light horse is fast and comfortable to ride. This is because of the shape of its body, with sloping shoulders and a back ideally suited to carrying a saddle. Once popular as a cavalry mount or for pulling coaches, today's light horses are used mostly for pleasure. Many modern breeds have been developed for this purpose.

Deep, compact body shape

COLORADO RANGER

COAT PATTERNS
Light horses come in a variety of colors and patterns – more so than ponies or heavy horses. The Colorado Ranger is a spotted breed. Its pattern is purely decorative and did not develop as camouflage.

LIGHT HORSE FACTS

• Some horses are famously hardy. In 1935, a group of Akhal Teke horses survived a ride of 600 miles (966 km) across the desert with little water.

• The vast herds of North American horses stemmed from 11 stallions and five mares brought over by Spanish conquistadors.

ORLOV TROTTER
This elegant breed was developed by Count Alexis Orlov in the 18th century. It is still raced in harness, but is not as fast as the American Standardbred.

CATTLE HORSES

The cowboy and his horse have long been synonymous with the North American West. The speed and agility of light horses made them well suited to rounding up sheep and cattle. Their endurance meant that they could cope with long trail rides.

Chaps protect the cowboy's legs from thorns

Palomino has a golden coat with a white mane and tail

Western bridle with curbed bit is of Spanish origin

SHAGYA ARAB

Some light horses were developed at breeding centers. The Shagya Arab comes from this stud farm at Babolna, Hungary. Early on, an Arab stallion called *Shagya* was involved in the breeding, giving the horses their name.

BARB

THE ANCESTORS OF this ancient horse were living in
North Africa as far back as the last ice age. The Barb
was taken to Europe by the Moors in the 7th century.
Some remained when the Moors left in the early 700s
and played a vital role
in the development
of today's breeds.

HEAD DETAIL
The wide muzzle is
nearly as broad as the
forehead. The narrow
skull is similar to the
early primitive
types such as
Przewalski's Horse.

*Head is long
and nose can
be curved.*

*Curved neck is
covered by long
flowing mane.*

*Shoulders
are flat and
upright.*

*Deep girth and
short, strong
back give the
breed its stamina.*

BARB FACTS

• The Barb was used in
battle for centuries and
is still ridden by Berber
tribes of North Africa.

• Traditionally, Barbs
are bay, dark bay, or
black in color. Gray
was introduced after
crossings with Arabians.

• More than a dozen of
today's breeds have
Barb blood in their
ancestries.

MASTER OF THE DESERT
The Barb is renowned
for its endurance and
copes well with heat and
drought. It is not a racehorse, but is fast over
short distances. The
Barb has Arabian blood,
and although there are
similarities, the Barb has
a heavier build.

15

COUNTRY OF ORIGIN
The Barb originally came from the Barbary coast in northwest Africa – hence the name.

Arched neck is carried proudly.

Strong shoulders

Hooves of tough blue horn

FRIESIAN
Evidence of the Barb's stamina and good character can be found in its relative, the Dutch Friesian. The black color and stylish movement of this breed made it a popular choice for pulling hearses in Europe during the 19th century.

Hooves are narrow and boxy.

Body is compact and short with well-sprung ribs.

Short, thick neck and powerful shoulders

LUSITANO
The Portuguese Lusitano was developed as a cavalry and coach horse during the 1500s. It inherited its agility from the Barb and still puts this to good use in the bullring.

THOROUGHBRED

THE FASTEST HORSE in the world is the Thoroughbred, and it is unlikely that a faster breed will ever be produced. This horse was developed in England during the 17th and 18th centuries especially for the sport of horse racing. Today, the Thoroughbred is at the center of a huge international industry and is bred in over 50 countries. It is also a major influence on many other competition breeds.

STUD FARMING
The first Thoroughbreds were produced when British running horses owned by the royal family were crossed with stallions from Turkey and Arabia. Thoroughbred stud farms have been around for over 200 years, and some stallions are worth a small fortune.

Powerful hindquarters

Long hind legs

Hard feet

QUICK COMPETITOR

Thoroughbreds start to race when only two years old, and most retire after about two years. They compete on flat ground or over fences, and can reach a speed of 40 mph (60 km/h). The first modern racecourse was set up in the 17th century near the English village of Newmarket.

UNIVERSAL APPEAL

All modern Thoroughbreds are descended from three stallions living in the mid-1700s. But it is only in the last 100 years that the breed has established its worldwide appeal.

Long, sloping shoulders help its easy galloping movement

Coat is fine and silky

Deep girth gives good lung capacity

Large joints

16

DUTCH WARMBLOOD

This breed of sports horse was developed in the Netherlands as recently as the 1960s. It is partly derived from the Thoroughbred, and careful breeding has made it a horse of the highest quality. Many are used for dressage.

Good muscle tone

PINTO AND PALOMINO

SOME HORSES are recognized as a breed because of their coloring. This is the case of the Pinto and Palomino which are strictly color types and not true breeds. The Palomino, has a distinctive golden coloring, while the two-colored coat of the Pinto is associated with many other horse and pony breeds. Both horses are much in demand for western trail rides.

RIDER AND PINTO

FAVOURITE MOUNT
The Pinto's camouflage coat made it a favourite mount of the Native Americans.

PALOMINO FACTS

• The Palomino is descended from the Spanish horses brought to the US by settlers in the 1500s.

• The name Palomino originates from Juan de Palomino, the Spanish Don, who was given a horse of this color.

• In Spain, the color palomino is sometimes called Ysabella after a queen who liked it.

Strong hindquarters make it a fast runner

The Overo pattern rarely has white legs

White is usually on the middle of the body

Markings allow individual horses to be distinguished easily

16

PALOMINO COLORING
The correct coloring is vital
for a Palomino to be registered
with the Palomino Horse
Association. Its coat is the
gold of a newly minted gold
coin, and can be only three
shades lighter or darker. Mane
and tail must be white.

*Silvery
white
mane*

*Body shape
influenced by
Spanish
ancestry*

16

*Thoroughbred
influence is visible
in the shape of
the head*

PINTO COLORING
The name Pinto comes from
the Spanish *pintado* (painted).
There are two color patterns,
Overo and Tobiano: Overo is
a colored coat with splashes of
white, Tobiano a white coat
with large patches of solid
color. The Sioux and Crow
Indians valued the Pinto for its
color and hardiness.

PALOMINO FEATURES
The tail of a
Palomino must
be white and
full. There
should be no
evidence of a
dorsal stripe
running down
the back.
White markings,
which are often
seen on the legs,
must not extend
above the knees,
or hocks.

*Full-length
silvery
white tail*

ARAB

FIERY AND COURAGEOUS, the Arab is not only the
purest of today's light horses, but it is also the
oldest, having been bred for
thousands of years. It has
influenced most other
horse breeds, especially
the Thoroughbred.

*Small ears are
sometimes
turned inwards*

ELEGANT ARAB
The Arab has an elegant appearance,
with a short head and dished face. Between the eyes
is a shield-shaped bulge called the "jibbah". The skin
around the muzzle is particularly soft. The large
nostrils help the horse to breathe easily when it is
running fast.

*Curved neck
allows the head
to turn freely*

*Tendons
are clearly
defined*

15

BEDOUINS AND THEIR HORSES
Bedouin Arabs have always been closely associated
with this "desert horse," which they tamed and
introduced into Europe during the 7th century.

BORN IN A LEGEND
Bedouin legend traces the
Arab back to a stallion
called Hoshaba. He was
mated with a mare called
Baz, who was said to
have been captured
by Bax, the great-
great-grandson of
Noah. Notes on
breeding and
feeding these
horses can be found
in the Koran.

COSSACK
RIDER

ARAB FACTS

• Napoleon rode his
gray Arab *Marengo* into
his final battle at
Waterloo in 1815.

• In the desert, these
horses will eat locusts,
meat, and dried dates.

• During the Crimean
War of 1851–4, one
Arab horse raced 93
miles (150 km) with no
ill effects, but the rider
died from exhaustion.

• The anatomy of the
Arab is unique, as it
has fewer vertebrae
than other horses.

*Tail is set high
and arches up
behind the body*

*Back is short
and slightly
curved*

*Slim, powerful legs
and sound hooves*

ENDURANCE HORSE
The Arab is famed for its powers of
endurance. In the 1800s, it was not
unknown for desert races to last for three
days. The Arab's stamina has made it a
popular choice for the growing sport of
endurance, trail, and long-distance riding.

ARAB WITH
SADDLE

QUARTER HORSE

THE FIRST ALL-AMERICAN horse, the Quarter Horse is not named for its well-muscled quarters. Instead, it got its name by racing over quarter-mile (400 m) distances, often down the main street of a town. Developed by the early New World settlers, it is still used on farms.

QUARTER HORSE FACTS
• The founder of the breed was an English Thoroughbred, kept in Virginia between 1756 and 1780.
• Quarter Horses still race in quarter-mile events, such as the All-American Futurity.

COLOR VARIATION
The colour of the Quarter Horse is influenced by its Spanish and Barb ancestors. They can be bred in any solid color, but most are chestnut. The horse below is a bay.

Heavily muscled thighs

Hind leg is perfectly formed

Underside of horse is longer than the back

Hard, well-formed joints

14

STRONG QUARTERS
Its powerful, massive quarters help the horse to sprint almost immediately from standing and increase its speed quickly.

WORKING HORSE
Roping cattle, whether on the range or competing in a rodeo, is dangerous and requires a sturdy mount. Quarter Horses are often used, since they are steady and work well under pressure. They are very agile horses and possess an almost instinctive ability to follow the twists and turns of a particular cow in a herd. This enables a rider to sit securely while concentrating on roping the target animal.

The shape of the back helps to hold the saddle firmly in place

Short, wide head

Small, very refined muzzle

Wide jawbones do not restrict breathing

orrectly ›d pasterns

MAIN FEATURES
The early Quarter Horses were part Thoroughbred and part Spanish. This produced a chunky, muscular look. Later, more Thoroughbred blood was used to make the breed faster and has given today's Quarter Horse a leaner appearance.

BUCKING BRONCO
A brave rodeo rider tries to hang on to an unbroken horse for as long as possible.

89

APPALOOSA

ONCE ALMOST EXTINCT, the American Appaloosa is now one of the most numerous horses in the world. It is distinguished by its spotted markings, although these also occur on other breeds. As a cattle horse, it showed its good stamina and easygoing nature. This has encouraged its use for racing and jumping.

HISTORY OF THE BREED

The Appaloosa is descended from spotted Spanish horses brought to America during the 16th century. During the 1700s, it was developed by the Nez Percé tribe of Native Americans in northeastern Oregon. When their territory was taken over by US troops in 1877, the tribe was pursued and the breed nearly wiped out.

Deep body with rounded ribs

APPALOOSA
AND RIDER

Blanket instead of saddle

BLANKET PATTERN

Tail is short to prevent it from getting caught on desert scrub

Black and white vertical stripes on hooves

15

HEAD DETAIL

An Appaloosa's head is often "hawk"-shaped. The skin on its nose, especially around the nostrils and the lips, is mottled with black and white spots. The white sclera of the eye is a breed characteristic. The registry was started in 1938 and within 50 years had over 400,000 horses.

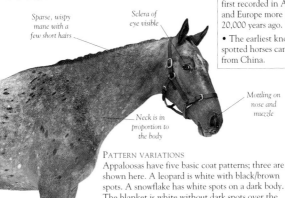

Sparse, wispy mane with a few short hairs

Sclera of eye visible

Mottling on nose and muzzle

Neck is in proportion to the body

PATTERN VARIATIONS

Appaloosas have five basic coat patterns; three are shown here. A leopard is white with black/brown spots. A snowflake has white spots on a dark body. The blanket is white without dark spots over the hips, a marble is mottled, and a frost has white specks on a dark background.

APPALOOSA CROSSBREED

LEOPARD PATTERN

ANDALUSIAN

ALSO KNOWN AS the Spanish Horse, this breed has
had great influence, particularly on the American
breeds. Its origins date back to the invasion of Spain
in A.D. 711 by the Berber Muslims
from North Africa, whose
Barb horses mixed with
Spanish ponies.

*Head curves
outward to give a
strong profile.*

*Dapple gray
coat*

*Strong, wide
shoulders*

15

ANDALUSIAN FACTS

• The Andalusian has
been used as the basis
for royal horses of many
countries including
Denmark, Austria,
Spain, and Britain.

• Andalusians were
used in Renaissance
riding schools.

• Today, the best
Andalusians stem from
those bred by the
Carthusian monks of
Jerez in Spain.

MAIN CHARACTERISTICS
The Andalusian's strong legs
and flexible joints give it a
relaxed but purposeful way of
walking. Today, most
Andalucians are bay or gray
in color, but in the past,
spotted and part-colored
horses existed.

Short, muscular neck is hidden by thick, wavy mane.

SORRAIA PONY INFLUENCE
These native Spanish ponies were mixed with Barbs from North Africa to produce the Andalusian. The hardy Sorraia resists both heat and cold, and was first tamed on the Iberian Peninsula, Europe.

Body shape is similar to that of the ancient Tarpan pony.

MANE POINT
An Andalusian can be recognized by its long, dense, and often wavy mane. This helps to show the neck's highly curved profile.

Decorative flowers

Special harness

SPANISH HORSE FESTIVAL
The home of the Andalusian is in southern Spain, particularly around Jerez de la Frontera, Cordoba, and Seville. Every year there is a horse fair in Jerez in which colorfully decorated horses are paraded through the streets. Andalusians are the traditional mount of the *rejoneadores* (Spanish bullfighters).

CLEVELAND BAY

DESCENDED FROM the Chapman Pack Horses of the Middle Ages, these powerful horses draw royal carriages on state occasions. Bred in the Cleveland area of northeast Yorkshire, they are characterized by a distinctive bay coat with black points, mane, and tail.

Curved and graceful neck

Muscular neck and sloping shoulders provide power

16

No feathering on the feet

ROYAL CARRIAGE HORSES
The Cleveland Bays used in England to pull the royal carriages are kept in the Royal Mews near Buckingham Palace in London. At one time, the Duke of Edinburgh raced a team of part Cleveland Bays in driving competitions.

INFLUENCES

The Cleveland Bay has been influenced by the imports of Spanish and Barb horses brought to the ports of north-east England in the 17th century from Spain and North Africa. It developed into the most powerful and important coach horse of Europe.

BAVARIAN WARMBLOOD

In the late 1700s, Cleveland Bays helped the development of the Bavarian Warmblood, giving it strength and stamina. This German breed is kept as a competition and carriage horse.

Tail is usually black, but gray hairs are a sign of purity

Powerful quarters help the horse to jump well

Legs are characterized by massive bone

CLEVELAND BAY FACTS

• In the Middle Ages, travelling salesmen (chapmen) originally used Clevelands as the Chapman Pack Horse.

• In 1962, Queen Elizabeth II bought and bred one of the last four stallions in order to save the breed from extinction.

• Cleveland Bays have been used as plow and draft horses on farms, as pack horses, and for carrying coal.

TRAKEHNER

ORIGINALLY DEVELOPED to take knights into battle, this horse has a long and colorful history. By the 16th century, the Trakehner was being refined into an elegant coach horse. Its bold and fearless nature made it useful for the cavalry. It is now highly valued in international sporting competitions.

Ears emphasize alert nature

Long, elegant neck

Face shows horse's similarity to Thoroughbred

Well-balanced body moves very freely

Strong legs and joints

16

COMPETITION FAVORITE

The Trakehner acquired its athletic and agile physique from earlier crossings with Thoroughbreds and Arabs. In the 1936 Berlin Olympics, the German team won every medal while riding Trakehners. Today, these horses have made a name for themselves in cross-country, jumping, and dressage events.

DRESSAGE COMPETITION

ELK-HORN BRAND

The Trakehner was once called the East Prussian because of its origins in what is now a part of Poland. The horses are distinguishable by the elk-horn brand on the nearside quarter.

ELK-HORN BRAND

Powerful quarters help jumping

TEUTONIC KNIGHTS

This ancient order of knights set up the site of the stud at Trakehnan in the 1200s to supply horses for the Crusades.

THE IDEAL HORSE

Today, many consider the Trakehner as being near to the ideal riding or competition horse, with good conformation and a temperament to match. It is highly courageous, and careful breeding has ensured that it has great stamina and endurance.

TRAKEHNER FACTS

• The breed's name comes from the site of the stud at Trakehnan, East Prussia.

• In 1945, over 1,000 Trakehners were led 900 miles (1,450 km) to western Germany to stop them being from captured by the advancing Russians.

LIPIZZANER

THESE BEAUTIFUL horses are usually associated with
the famous Spanish Riding School in Vienna – so
called because it has always used Spanish horses.
The Lipizzaner has been developed as a classical
riding horse from five stallions brought from Spain
during the 16th century by Archduke Charles II,
ruler of the Austro-Hungarian Empire.

*Broad, powerful
quarters are a
feature of the
breed*

*Compact and
muscular body
with a deep chest*

*Firm joints and
hard grooves*

LIPIZZANER AND RIDER
At the Spanish Riding School in Vienna,
Lipizzaners are trained over a period of 4–6
years to perform the classical movements
of the High School. Lipizzaners may also
be used in harness but it is unusual to see
them ridden sidesaddle.

Shoulders are well suited to harness riding

AUSTRIAN STUD
The Lipizzaners at the Spanish Riding School are bred at Piber, near Graz, Austria. Eight to ten horses are selected each year.

LIPIZZANER FACTS
• There are about 3,500 Lipizzaner horses in the world.

• The breed is named after the original stud at Lipiza in Slovenia, then part of Austria.

• The horses are a select breed and all are descended from one of five stallions.

Ramlike profile of the Andalusian is still evident

COLOR CHANGES
Adult Lipizzaners bred at Piber should be all white, but foals are dark brown or black at birth. The horses grow lighter as they mature between the ages of seven and ten. Color variations at other studs are quite common.

White mare and dark brown foal

Short, powerful legs

16

AUSTRALIAN STOCK HORSE

TOUGH AND VERSATILE, the Stock Horse was bred to work under the harsh conditions of the Australian outback. Similar horses have been kept on cattle stations there for nearly 200 years, yet even today the Australian Stock Horse is not considered a standardized breed.

Head is heavy and chunky compared to a Thoroughbred's

Most Stock Horses are bay, but other colours are seen occasionally

STOCK HORSE FACTS

• *Regal Realm*, a famous World Event champion, had a Stock Horse background.

• Stock Horses make up the largest single group of horses in Australia.

• Over 12,000 Walers, sent to fight in World War I, were destroyed after the war ended. Australia's strict quarantine laws prevented their return.

Sloping shoulders are a sign of a good riding horse

Good, sloped pasterns

RECENT BREED
After World War I, there were few horses left in Australia to work on the farms. Some of these horses were crossed with Thoroughbreds and Arabs, giving rise to the Stock Horse. It is still not accepted as a standard breed because of this mixture.

COUNTRY OF ORIGIN
Ancestors of the
Australian Stock Horse
were nicknamed Walers
after the southeastern
state of New South Wales
where they worked.

CHARGE OF THE AUSTRALIAN LIGHT HORSES
During World War I, the British General, Allenby,
used Walers in his campaign against the Turks in
Palestine with great success. A troop of these horses
covered 170 miles (274 km) in four days, while
temperatures reached 100°F (37.8°C).

Powerful
hindquarters

Well-
proportioned
legs

16

This Australian Stock
Horse shows Arab
influence

OUTBACK WORK
Rounding up stray
cattle and sheep on
the vast stations of
Australia calls for a
breed with stamina
and endurance. The
first horses brought to
Australia came from
South Africa and then
from Europe. These
were superb riding
horses that could stand
up to the heat.

MORGAN AND DUTCH WARMBLOOD

THESE TWO BREEDS were developed as versatile all-rounders. The Morgan ancestry dates from the late 18th century, whilst the Dutch Warmblood has evolved during the present century as a competition horse.

MORGAN STATUE
The Morgan is much revered in the US. This statue is in the Kentucky Horse Park.

Fine muzzle, with small, firm lips and large nostrils

15

Colors are either bay, brown, black, or chestnut

Wide, deep chest

Long, flowing tail should reach the ground

Ample bone beneath the knee

FIRST MORGAN
The founding stallion of the breed, *Figure*, was born in about 1790 at West Springfield, Massachussetts. In local contests, whether pulling logs or racing, the horse would beat all challengers.

DRESSAGE RIDER
ON DUTCH
WARMBLOOD

MORGAN FACTS

• *Figure* was later called *Justing Morgan*, after his owner. He died in 1821 at 32 years of age.

• These horses are very versatile and are used for driving, jumping, and dressage.

• Both the American Saddlebred and the Tennessee Walking horses were influenced by the Morgan.

COMPETITION HORSES

The Dutch Warmblood was developed from coach horse breeds, but the subsequent Thoroughbred crosses have resulted in competition horses excelling at dressage and jumping.

Head shape is similar to a Thoroughbred's

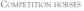

16

Common colors are brown and bay

Deep body and long back

DUTCH WARMBLOOD
This horse is a mix of the Dutch Groningen and Gelderlander. The Warmblood was bred specifically to take part in competitions. Famous horses include *Dutch Courage* and Milton.

Good, sound hooves

Well-rounded hooves

HEAVY HORSES

INTRODUCTION TO
HEAVY HORSES 106

JUTLAND 108

BRABANT 110

PERCHERON 112

CLYDESDALE 114

SUFFOLK PUNCH 116

SHIRE 118

ARDENNAIS 120

INTRODUCTION TO HEAVY HORSES

THE SHEER SIZE and power of the heavy horses makes them instantly recognizable. They include the largest and tallest horses ever bred. Heavy horses have a wide body and a broad back. The shoulders are upright, allowing them to be fitted with a collar, while the chest is broad and powerful.

THE WORKING HORSES
Before mechanization became widespread, heavy horses were very much part of everyday life. Draft, or pulling, horses were harnessed to all kinds of vehicles, from wagons like the one shown here to the first buses and trams. Horses also provided muscle power in factories.

Most heavy horses have feathering on their feet

ITALIAN HEAVY HORSE

Most heavy horses were developed to be strong and to move at a steady pace. The Italian Heavy Horse was mixed with French and English breeds, and is used for light draft work in northern and central Italy.

Body of draft horse is compact and muscular

FORESTRY WORK

Heavy horses are still used in forests around the world for hauling timber. Forestry work is performed better by heavy horses than vehicles, as horses cause less damage to the ground and do not need wide tracks to get into the forest.

PLOW HORSES

Horses have been used for plowing the land since about AD 500, when the Chinese invented a special padded collar for this purpose. This made the heavy horse important to countries that relied on farming for much of their economy.

JUTLAND

CARRYING HEAVILY ARMORED knights into battle was
all part of a day's work for the Jutland in medieval
times. On more peaceful occasions, this Danish breed
was employed on farms, plowing fields and hauling
heavy loads over rough tracks. However,
increased mechanization means
that today Jutlands are rarely
seen working the land.

*Solid, heavy
hindquarters*

*Deep
girth*

*Joints are
round and
fleshy*

16

STILL IN HARNESS
The Jutland is ideally suited to
pulling heavy loads. Although no
longer common on farms, some are
still used to pull brewers' dray carts
through the streets of Denmark.

COAT OF DARK COLORS
The Jutland's dark chestnut coat and flaxen mane and tail are the result of crossings with the Suffolk Punch that first took place over 100 years ago.

Head is plain and heavy

Strong, powerful shoulders

Legs are shorter than the girth

HEAVY FEATHERING
Excess hair above the hooves can become soiled by mud, causing disease. Regular cleaning is needed to prevent this.

COUNTRY OF ORIGIN
These heavy horses are named after Denmark's Jutland Peninsula, where they were first bred over 1,000 years ago. They have been carefully developed there ever since.

JUTLAND FACTS
• Viking invaders brought the forerunners of the Jutland to Britain during the 900s.

• Modern Jutlands can be traced to a British Suffolk Punch taken to Denmark in 1860.

• A few Jutlands have coats colored black, bay, or roan.

• Though undesirable, the heavy feathering on the leg is an easy way to tell the Jutland from the Suffolk Punch.

BRABANT

THE HEAVIEST OF the heavy horses, the Brabant is also known as the Belgian Draft. This gentle giant was bred in Europe, but has gained huge popularity in the US since it was first exported there in the 19th century. Brabants have also played a major part in the development of other heavy breeds, such as the English Suffolk Punch.

DIFFERENT TYPES
By the 1870s, there were three groups of Brabants: the *Colosses de la Mahaique* is the most powerful, the *Gris du Hainaut* has a distinctive red roan coloring, and the *Gros de la Dendre* is smaller and lighter than the others.

Huge, rounded hindquarters

Thick-set compact body, with a very deep girth

Medium-sized hooves are well formed

Short, sturdy legs

BRABANT FACTS

• The world's heaviest a Brabant was the American stallion, *Brooklyn Supreme*, who, in 1937, weighed in at 3,200 lb (1,451 kg).

• The Brabant is also called the *race de trait Belge* by the Belgians.

• A heavily pregnant Brabant mare was measured as having a 12 ft (3.65 m) girth.

17

Strong and sturdy
An exceedingly strong horse, the Brabant has a tremendously robust, yet short, back and loins. It has huge muscles, important for a draft horse since it spends most of its working life in harness. These characteristics have been carefully maintained by selective breeding.

Long, thick mane

Country of origin
The Brabant was named after the plains area of Flanders in Belgium where it was developed. Many are now bred in America.

Broad chest and short neck

Head is small compared to other heavy horses

Some feathering on lower leg

Working the land
The Brabant was once the most famous heavy horse in Europe. During medieval times, it became known as the Flanders Horse and was much in demand as a plow horse. Suited to the variable Belgian climate and working the rich, heavy soil, this colossus was also used to pull farm wagons or dray carts in towns.

PERCHERON

ONE OF THE LARGEST and most elegant of the heavy horses is the French Percheron. It has been used in battle, on farms, as a coach horse, and, in spite of its size, has even been ridden for pleasure. Its strength and willing nature has led to many being exported to work all over the world.

Arched neck is covered by a thick mane.

Fine head shape with square, straight profile

Flat nose with broad, open nostrils

Shoulders are unusually long for a heavy horse.

Broad, very deep-chested body

Medium-sized hooves of hard blue horn

PERCHERON FACTS

• The world's biggest horse was an American Percheron, Dr. Le Gear, who was 21 hh and weighed 3,024 lb (1,372 kg) in 1908.

• A lighter version of the Percheron was used to haul horse-drawn Paris buses in the late 19th century.

• Percherons can pull loads of more than 2,205 lb (1,000 kg).

STRENGTH AND BEAUTY
The Percheron's refined shape comes from its crossings with Barb and Arabian horses, brought to Europe from North Africa by Moorish invaders in A.D. 300. Later, Belgian horses helped to give the breed

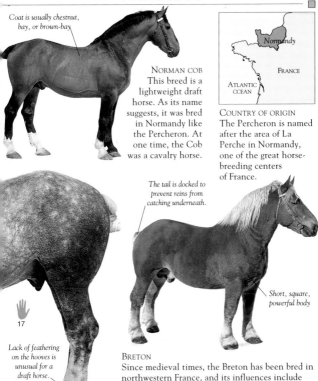

Coat is usually chestnut, bay, or brown-bay

NORMAN COB
This breed is a lightweight draft horse. As its name suggests, it was bred in Normandy like the Percheron. At one time, the Cob was a cavalry horse.

COUNTRY OF ORIGIN
The Percheron is named after the area of La Perche in Normandy, one of the great horse-breeding centers of France.

The tail is docked to prevent reins from catching underneath.

17

Lack of feathering on the hooves is unusual for a draft horse.

Short, square, powerful body

BRETON
Since medieval times, the Breton has been bred in northwestern France, and its influences include both the Percheron and Ardennais. The Breton is used on farms, especially in the vineyards of the Midi region of France. There were once several types of Breton, but only two survive today.

CLYDESDALE

POWERFUL HORSES did most of the plowing and heavy work on farms before the days of the steam engine. The Clydesdale was specially bred for this purpose and was exported from Britain to countries all around the world. It is regarded as one of the strongest of the heavy horses.

Long, muscular hindquarters

Head profile is straight and elegant

17

Hooves covered by heavy, silky feathering

GOOD MOVER
At one time, the Clydesdale was seen as a type of Shire Horse. Although not as big, the Clydesdale shares the Shire's lively, stylish way of moving.

BREED FOUNDER
The Clydesdale was developed in the 18th century by the sixth Duke of Hamilton and another breeder, John Paterson. Together, they imported Flemish horses to increase the size and power of the local draught breeds. Later, Shire mares were also involved.

SIXTH DUKE OF HAMILTON

COUNTRY OF ORIGIN
The natural home of the Clydesdale is the Clyde Valley in Lanarkshire, Scotland. Although no longer at work on farms there, some Clydesdales still work in forests in Canada and the Russian Federation.

The rider's uniform is embroidered with gold thread

Silver drums weigh 150 lb (68 kg) each

SOUNDS OF WAR
This drum horse is a 15-year-old blue roan Clydesdale. The beating of drums once inspired soldiers as they went into battle, but today the role of the drum horse is ceremonial. These two silver drums were presented to the Household Cavalry of Great Britain by King William IV in 1830.

The rider steers by reins connected to boots and waist

CLYDESDALE FACTS
• The heaviest and tallest Clydesdale ever recorded weighed 2,800 lb (1,270 kg) and was 20 hh.

• In Michigan, one horse pulled a load of nearly 50 tons (tonnes) over a distance of 1,320 ft (402 m).

• In the days before mechanization, wheat farmers in Canada used teams of about seven horses to pull three-furrowed plows.

SUFFOLK PUNCH

THE TERM "PUNCH" is an old English name for a horse with a barrel-shaped body and short legs. The Suffolk Punch is the oldest of Britain's heavy horses. It was developed in the eastern county of Suffolk during the 1700s. Today, every one of these horses can trace its ancestry back to the first Suffolk, foaled in 1768. The color of the breed is traditionally described "chesnut," without the use of the first "t."

Suffolks are bred in seven shades; this example is red.

WORKING HORSES
The Suffolk Punch was developed as a farm horse, well suited to working the heavy clay soils of eastern England. In spite of its bulk, it can walk a furrow just 9 in (23 cm) wide. The horses are economical to keep and have long, productive lives, with some continuing to work into their twenties.

Lack of feathering keeps mud from clinging to lower leg

HINDQUARTERS
The immense strength of the
Suffolk is partly due to its short
legs and wide body. When the
horse is working, its tail is often
braided in this way to keep it
clear of any machinery.

*Hindquarters
have a great deal
of power.*

*Legs are short
and muscular.*

*This mane is braided,
ready for a show.*

*The powerful
neck is deep and
muscular.*

*Small ears for
a heavy horse.*

GOOD NATURED
The modern
Suffolk Punch
is a big and
impressive horse,
with a docile and
obliging nature.

*Low shoulders
aid the horse's
pulling power.*

*Feet are small
compared to
other heavy
horses.*

16

JUTLAND

The modern Jutland is descended
from a Suffolk Punch exported to
Denmark in 1860. This Danish breed
is still kept as a working horse and
retains characteristics of its
English relative, such as its
very rounded quarters.

*Heavy
feathering
on hooves.*

SHIRE

THE LARGEST OF ALL modern horse breeds, the Shire, is descended from the English Great Horses which were used in medieval times to carry heavily armored knights into battle. The name "Shire" comes from the Midland shire counties of England, from where its ancestors originated.

HEAD DETAIL
The shoulders of the Shire are wide and deep. The neck is quite long for a draft horse, and slightly arched. A broad forehead, separates the large, docile eyes that give the Shire its "gentle giant" look.

Back is short and strong.

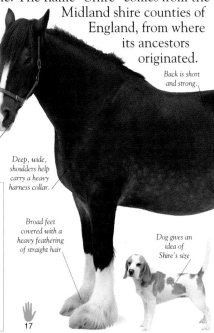

Nose is slightly curved

Deep, wide, shoulders help carry a heavy harness collar.

Broad feet covered with a heavy feathering of straight hair

Dog gives an idea of Shire's size

SHIRE FACTS

• In the 1500s, the Shire was influenced by Flanders horses brought to drain the swampy English fenland.

• In 1924, a pair showed a pulling power of 50 tons (tonnes).

• Young Shires are able to work by the time they are three.

17

CART HORSES

Until the mid-1880s, the Shire was known as the English Cart Horse. Its power made it much in demand for pulling carts and working the land. Most Shires can pull loads of up to five tons (tonnes) without difficulty. Today, they can still be seen in English cities, working as draft horses for breweries.

In the country, Shires appear at agricultural shows in plowing competitions.

SHIRE HORSE
AND CART

Broad, well-muscled hindquarters

QUICK DEVELOPERS

A Shire has to be at least 16.2 hands high to be registered. It takes around six years for a Shire to grow to its maximum size, with stallions tending to be taller than mares. One Shire, foaled in 1846, grew to more than 21.2 hh by the time it was four and weighed almost 3,360 lb (1,524 kg).

SHIRE
MARE

SHIRE
FOAL

ARDENNAIS

THIS BREED IS regarded as the founder of the European draft horses. It is also called the Ardennes, after the area between France and Belgium where its ancestors lived over 2,000 years ago. One of the oldest heavy breeds, the Ardennais has put its tremendous strength to use on both the farm and the battlefield.

Thick hair on mane

Squared-off, snub nose

Heavy, muscular neck is set back into the shoulders

ARDENNAIS FACTS

• Julius Caesar wrote about this horse in his accounts of the Roman conquest of northern France in 51 BC.

• An artillery horse, it is a veteran of both the French Revolution and World War I.

• The two main types are the heavyweight Ardennais du Nord and the powerful Auxois.

BODY CHARACTERISTICS
The Ardennais has a low, flat forehead that gives it a straight profile. The ears are pricked in an alert manner and the eye sockets are prominent. The wide frame and short legs give an impression of compact strength and power.

Dense feathering above small but powerful feet

ARDENNAIS
ON SHOW

WILLING WORKERS
The Ardennais are
gentle horses and are
managed easily. They
are still hard at work on
farms in the Ardennes,
where the harsh winters
have made them tough.
Their ancestors were used
by Napoleon's army to
carry supplies.

*Compact and stocky
body shape, with a short
back and quarters*

*Limbs like tree
trunks – thick,
short, and
strong*

BOULONNAIS

Like the Ardennais, the
Boulonnais is also descended
from the ancient Forest Horse
and developed in northwestern
France. However, its Arab blood
has given the Boulonnais an
elegant appearance, described
as looking like polished
marble. Most are gray,
but others are bay
or chestnut.

16

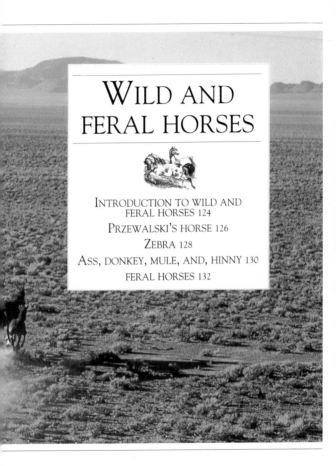

WILD AND
FERAL HORSES

INTRODUCTION TO WILD AND
FERAL HORSES 124

PRZEWALSKI'S HORSE 126

ZEBRA 128

ASS, DONKEY, MULE, AND, HINNY 130

FERAL HORSES 132

INTRODUCTION TO WILD AND FERAL HORSES

FOUR DIFFERENT GROUPS of horses live in the wild: the true wild horses, zebras, asses, and feral (semiwild) horses. All these species are grazing animals that live in herds. Sadly, though domestic horses have thrived, hunting and the destruction of their habitat have made wild horses increasingly scarce.

DÜLMEN PONY
Some ponies, like the European Dülmen, have roamed in a semiwild state for centuries. Members of this breed have lived at Mierfelder Bruch in Westphalia, Germany since 1316. Although Dülmens resemble the British New Forest Pony, there is no link between the two breeds.

ZEBRAS
All three types of zebras live in Africa. They are easily recognized by their black and white stripes, which serve as a form of camouflage.

kulans can go 2–3 days without water

Kulans can run at speeds up to 40 mph (65 km/h)

KULAN ASSES

Wild asses live in Africa and Asia. They prefer dry, stony habitats, where they feed on grass and shrubs. Kulans are a subspecies of onagers and live in small numbers in Turkmenistan, east of the Caspian Sea.

WILD HORSE FACTS

• Herds of wild asses have been known to number upto 1000 animals.

• Not all zebras have stripes; some are pure black. Although rare, these live alongside their striped cousins.

• Wild horses usually spend 60–80 percent of their time looking for food.

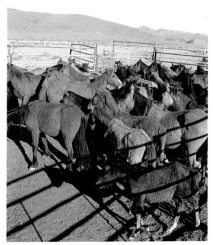

FERAL HORSES

In some places, domestic horses that escaped into the wild have formed feral herds. These animals are rounded up occasionally to check their health.

PRZEWALSKI'S HORSE

THIS ASIAN WILD horse was discovered
in 1881 by a Russian colonel, who
gave the breed its name. It is an
important link between the early
types of wild horse and today's
modern breeds.

RUSSIAN EXPLORER
Colonel N.M. Przewalski
(1839-88) was a Russian
soldier and explorer. By
the time he made his
discovery, the horse
was already in
decline; it was
extinct in the
wild by 1969.

Sparse, short
mane grows
upright and
is always
partly black .

Short forelock
does not
reach eyes.

13

Dark, zebralike
markings on
lower leg

Colored speckles
on muzzle and
around eyes

CAPTIVE SURVIVORS
In 1900, Przewalski's Horses were first kept at the
Askania-Nova Zoo, in the Ukraine – where the
largest group lives today. In 1959, a breeding
program was started, with the goal of
reestablishing these horses in the wild.
Today, there are more than 600
Prezwalski's horses worldwide.

PRZEWALSKI FACTS
• Przewalski foals are a
shade of yellowish
brown at birth but are
dun (dusky) colored by
the time they are adults.
• A frozen carcass
15,000 years old has
been found in the
northern part of the
Russian Federation.
• A herd is led by
the most dominant
stallion, which is at
least 10 years old.

AREA OF DISCOVERY
Przewalski discovered
this horse in the area of
the Tachin Schah (the
"Mountains of the
Yellow Horses") on the
edge of the Gobi Desert.

TARPAN
This illustration shows a Tarpan, another Asian
wild horse. Although extinct in the wild by 1879,
some were kept and crossbred by Polish farmers.
Recently, horses with the greatest likeness to their
ancestors have helped recreate semiwild herds.

ZEBRA

THE STRIPED PATTERN of the
zebra makes it instantly
recognizable. All three types of
zebra live in Africa, but in
different areas. Grevy's zebras can
be found in the far north, the
Plains zebras roam the grasslands to
the east, and the Mountain zebras
inhabit the uplands of the south.

GREVY'S ZEBRA
This is the largest zebra,
standing 5 ft (1.6 m) tall
at the shoulder. It is an
endangered species –
only about 7,000 remain.

*Striped coat helps
individual zebras blend
together in a herd*

ZEBRA FACTS

• Zebras have good
hearing, but they also
rely on nearby animals
– ostriches for sight and
wildebeest for smell –
to help warn them of
approaching danger.

• Zebras defend
themselves from
predators such as lions
by lashing out with
their feet.

• Mountain zebras are
very rare and may soon
be extinct.

*A young zebra is
fully developed and
can run within
hours of its birth.*

*Powerful legs allow
a zebra to reach
25 mph (40 km/h)*

PLAINS ZEBRA
These are the most common zebras, and herds can still be seen in most African wildlife reserves. Zebras look after each other and if one member of the group goes missing, the others will search for it.

Mane stands up on back of neck

Mare and foal stay together for about five months

TAME ZEBRAS
A few zebras have been trained to pull carriages. This 19th-century scene shows a team of four zebras pulling a trader's vehicle, but these examples were usually gimmicks performed by publicity-conscious companies. In rare cases, zebras have known to be broken and ridden.

QUAGGA
A close relative of the zebra, the quagga lived in southern Africa. During the 1840s, these animals were hunted heavily for their meat and hides. The last survivor died in Amsterdam Zoo in 1883.

ASS, DONKEY, MULE, AND HINNY

PAIRINGS OF HORSES and wild asses have been carried out for centuries to produce working animals that are strong, yet more sure-footed than the horse. The donkey is the domesticated form of the African wild ass. A mule has a donkey father and a horse mother. A hinny has a horse father and donkey mother.

Shaggy coat

Light-colored underside

Short brown mane

Light-colored legs blend into the background.

WORKING DONKEYS
Donkeys are very strong and have been used for pulling carts in Ireland for centuries. To help them cope with the colder northern climate, these donkeys have grown thick coats.

AFRICAN WILD ASS
The ass is the ancestor of the donkey. These asses live in herds in hot, dry regions of northern Africa.

EUROPEAN DONKEY AND CART

130

DOMESTIC DONKEYS
Many donkeys are kept as pets. They are social animals and should not be kept alone.

Large ears

Muscular neck and heavy head

Strong, sturdy legs

Mule's stubbornness stems from its wariness of people.

Hooves can become overgrown if the donkey lives at pasture.

MULE
Mules were first bred in the Middle East about 4,000 years ago. They have strong herd instincts and so work better in packs than by themselves. These groups are called mule trains.

Mane is closer in shape to a donkey's than a horse's.

HINNY
Hinnies live for up to 40 years. Although they are usually sterile, on occasion they have been known to produce foals.

Color can vary

DONKEY FACTS
• Donkeys bred in the Poitou region of France and Spain are among the largest in the world at 56 in (142 cm).
• The largest donkey ever recorded lived in Glasgow, Scotland, in 1902, and was 84 in (213 cm) high.
• Miniature donkeys less than 34 in (86 cm) tall live on the Mediterranean islands of Sardinia and Sicily.

FERAL HORSES

DOMESTIC ANIMALS that have returned to the wild are described as feral. Many horses around the world have either escaped from their owners or have been abandoned. If they remain uncontrolled, feral horses can cause great damage through overgrazing and trampling on crops.

CHRISTOPHER COLUMBUS
The early American feral horses were descendants of Spanish horses taken to the New World by Columbus in 1493.

CAMARGUES
These white horses live in the coastal marshes of the Rhône delta, southern France, where they survive on a meager, salty diet. They are ridden by French *gardians* (cowboys).

FERAL FACTS

• There were an estimated five million feral horses in the US in the late 16th century.

• Small, dun-colored feral horses living in Colombia are possibly descendants of horses brought by the Spanish conquistadors.

• Camargues are sometimes called "the horses of the sea."

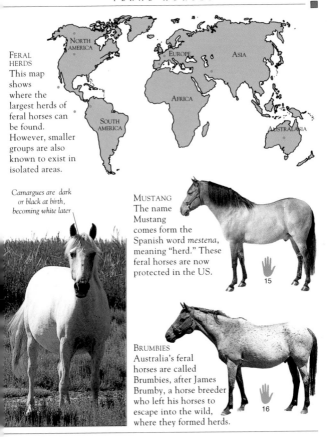

FERAL HERDS
This map shows where the largest herds of feral horses can be found. However, smaller groups are also known to exist in isolated areas.

Camargues are dark or black at birth, becoming white later

MUSTANG
The name Mustang comes form the Spanish word *mestena*, meaning "herd." These feral horses are now protected in the US.

15

BRUMBIES
Australia's feral horses are called Brumbies, after James Brumby, a horse breeder who left his horses to escape into the wild, where they formed herds.

16

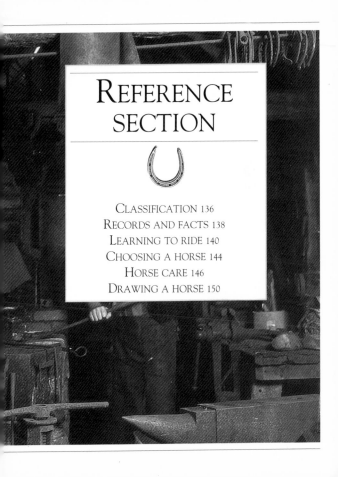

REFERENCE
SECTION

CLASSIFICATION 136
RECORDS AND FACTS 138
LEARNING TO RIDE 140
CHOOSING A HORSE 144
HORSE CARE 146
DRAWING A HORSE 150

HORSE CLASSIFICATION

WITHIN THE GROUP of animals known as mammals horses form part of a smaller group, the *Perissodactyla* or odd-toed mammals. Members of this group include rhinoceroses, with three toes on each limb, as well as single-hooved horses. Within this category, zebras, asses, and horses make up a small family called Equidae. Each species can breed with other members of the family and their offspring are called hybrids.

MULE

PART OF THE FAMILY
Although part of the horse family Equidae, the mule is classified as a hybrid. In most cases, hybrids are sterile. Ponies are grouped with domestic horses, as they can breed with horses and produce fertile offspring.

HYBRIDS
These are offspring that have parents from different species. Some crosses are deliberate, with the goal of combining the qualities of both parents. Zebroids, for example, may be more suitable for working in the hot African climate than are horses.

MALE DONKEY	+	FEMALE HORSE	=	MULE
MALE HORSE	+	FEMALE DONKEY	=	HINNY
ZEBRA	+	HORSE	=	ZEBROID
ZEBRA	+	DONKEY	=	ZEDONK

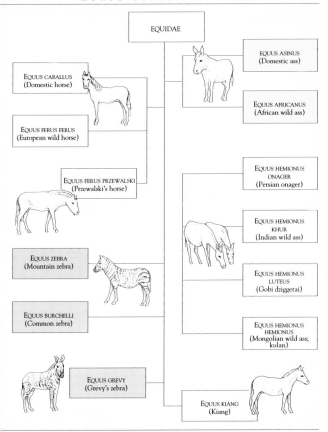

EQUIDAE

EQUUS CABALLUS
(Domestic horse)

EQUUS FERUS FERUS
(European wild horse)

EQUUS FERUS PRZEWALSKI
(Przewalski's horse)

EQUUS ZEBRA
(Mountain zebra)

EQUUS BURCHELLI
(Common zebra)

EQUUS GREVY
(Grevy's zebra)

EQUUS ASINUS
(Domestic ass)

EQUUS AFRICANUS
(African wild ass)

EQUUS HEMIONUS
ONAGER
(Persian onager)

EQUUS HEMIONUS
KHUR
(Indian wild ass)

EQUUS HEMIONUS
LUTEUS
(Gobi dziggetai)

EQUUS HEMIONUS
HEMIONUS
(Mongolian wild ass;
kulan)

EQUUS KIANG
(Kiang)

RECORDS AND FACTS

THE SHEER DIVERSITY of horse types and breeds
spread around the world has led to a number of
quite amazing facts and figures. Although some are
natural phenomena, many are connected with the
horse's association with people, a relationship that
goes back over 6,000 years.

• The tallest known
horse was an English
Shire called *Mammoth*,
which stood at 21.2
hands high.

• The US Pony Express
ran from Missouri to
California, a distance of
1,966 miles (3,164 km).
This was covered by
400 ponies in a relay
over 10 days.

• When spoken to,
horses distinguish tones
rather than particular
words.

• Shetland pit ponies
worked underground for
around 20 years.

• The oldest known
Thoroughbred was a
chestnut gelding called
Tango Duke. It was
born in 1935 in
Victoria, Australia and
lived for 42 years.

• The game of polo
originated in Persia
over 2,500 years ago
and was played by both
men and women.

• The smallest and
lightest horse in the
world was reckoned to
be *Little Pumpkin*, a
miniature horse foaled
in the US in 1973.
When two years old, it
was 3.5 hands high and
weighed just
over 20 lb
(9 kg).

• The heaviest weight
ever pulled by two
horses was recorded in
1893, when two
Clydesdales pulled a
load weighing 131 tons
(tonnes). But recent
estimates put
the load at about
50 tons (tonnes).

• The most recently
discovered breed was
the Caspian pony,
found in Iran in 1965.

• In 1277, a *destrier*, or
trained battle charger,
cost roughly the
equivalent of a modern
limousine. Less
powerful horses were
only a third as much.

- Horses can breed throughout their lives. The oldest horse ever to give birth was a 42 year-old Australian brood mare.

- The longest mane belonged to a horse from California, called *Maud*. It grew to a length of 18 ft (5.5 m).

- Today there are over 150 different horse and pony breeds, as well as many crossbred types.

- The longest tail, measuring 22 ft (6.7 m), was grown by an American Palomino called *Chinook*.

- The top-earning movie horse

was *Tony* "the Wonder Horse." With cowboy film star Tom Mix (1880–1940), Tony earned around $8 million in almost 300 films until injury ended his career in 1932.

- Zebras have stripes that evolved originally as camouflage to break up the body outline.

- Horses were first used for public transportation in Britain in 1564.

- The first recorded race with mounted horses was at the Greek Olympiad in 624 BC.

- Horses were first shod in Roman times by Celtic mercenaries.

- In England, people drive cars on the left. This custom stems from coaching days, when drivers drove on the left to prevent their whip (which was held in the right hand) becoming entangled in hedgerows bordering the side of the road.

- Horses have two blind spots. One is directly behind them and the other is right in front of the end of their nose.

- The last horse-drawn passenger train ran over the Fintona branch line in Northern Ireland, which closed in 1957.

- Rodeos began in the 19th century as informal contests between American cowboys. The first attempt to stage a world cup rodeo contest was in 1982, in Australia.

- Genghis Khan operated the Yam – mounted messengers who crossed the Mongol Empire, covering 150 miles (242 km) a day.

- Millions of acres of American farmland were harvested with huge machines drawn by teams of up to 24 horses.

- In 1286 BC at the battle of Kadesh, in present-day Syria, the Hittites used 3,500 horsedrawn chariots in their defeat of Rameses I of Egypt.

LEARNING TO RIDE

RIDING CAN BE ENJOYED at any level, from a gentle hack in the country to taking part in national competitions. The rider progresses through different stages and learns how to control the horse while developing balance and rhythm. Having a good instructor and learning the correct methods from the start is the best way to begin.

RIDING SCHOOL
The ideal place to learn to ride is at a registered riding school with qualified instructors who can help riders correct their mistakes quickly.

EQUIPMENT
Riders should dress for safety and comfort. Some special items may be needed for riding in the dark. 1 Warm jumper for cold weather. 2 Tweed hacking jacket for everyday wear. 3 Hard hat covered with silk. 4 Stretch jodhpurs for freedom of movement. 5 Jodhpur boots. 6 Long leather, or rubber boots. 7 Gloves. 8 Stirrup light. 9 Fluorescent belt for night riding. 10 Cross-country whip.

MOUNTING UP

1 Stand on left of horses facing tail. Hold reins in left hand placed in front of saddle and turn stirrup iron outward.

2 Put left foot into stirrup iron and face horse's side. Hold bottom of mane with right hand and push off ground with right leg.

3 Swing right leg over horse's back, turn body to face forward and lower body into saddle. Place right foot in stirrup iron.

Back is upright but relaxed; arm follows the movement of horse's head

The pressure on the horse's mouth is called the contact

LEADING ON A REIN
It takes time for the novice rider to get used to the movement of the horse. The instructor will help by leading the horse, leaving the rider to settle into the rhythm.

Leading rein

Long schooling whip

Stirrup iron should be under the ball of the foot

Horse has a relaxed pace

The different gaits

A horse moves its legs in a different sequence for each change of pace, from a trot to a canter to a gallop. Riders must learn to keep their body movements in time with the rhythm of the horse.

TROT

CANTER

Sit deeply in the saddle

Keep the rein in contact with horse's mouth

GALLOP

Stirrups must be shortened

JUMPING

The secret of a successful jump lies in the approach, with a confident and correctly balanced rider. The rider must wait for the horse to take off before leaning forward. The horse must have enough speed and not be restricted by the reins as it jumps.

Sit still on approach

Keep hands still

TROT
The trot is quite a bumpy movement. Riders learn to let the horse throw them up in the saddle and land back lightly.

Press with the inside of the legs to help keep horse moving

CANTER
The rider's back is relaxed to move in harmony with the rocking motion of the horse. The hands follow the movement of the horse's head.

Lean forward from the hips

Hands stay on either side of neck

GALLOP
The rider sits forward and rises slightly out of the saddle to take the weight off the horse's back, allowing it to go faster.

Keep head up and eyes straight ahead

Make sure lower legs are held straight under the body

CHOOSING A HORSE

OWNING A HORSE requires considerable commitment, both in time and money. The horse must above all be suitable for the purpose in mind. It is better to buy privately rather than at an auction since this allows a closer inspection. The horse should be ridden and then checked closely by a vet before a final decision is made.

FURTHER EXPENSES
Apart from the cost of the horse, there will be stabling, food, and veterinary bills. You will also need to buy equipment, such as tack and clothing.

9–10 YEARS   15 YEARS

19–20 YEARS   20–25 YEARS

TEETH
The front teeth can be used to tell the age of a horse. As the horse ages, the slope of the teeth increases and they become discolored.

Saddle must fit properly

Riding clothing can be expensive

Horses need to be shod every four to six weeks

WHAT TO LOOK FOR

NOSE
The nostrils should have large air passages and be thin and flexible. When the horse is at rest, they should be almost closed. If not, there could be a breathing problem.

EYES
Poor eyesight can cause a horse to shy away from things. The eyes should be clear and free from tears, the pupils black, and the eyelids thin and smooth.

TEETH
The front teeth should be level; otherwise, the horse will be unable to graze properly. Check for damage in the mouth caused by an unsuitable bit or sharp teeth.

HOOFS
The wall of the hoof should be smooth, not cracked or brittle. The hoof must be symmetrical, with the shoes worn evenly – an uneven fit might indicate a defect.

LEGS
The tendons should be hard and sinewy and not soft and puffy. Soreness or swelling is a sign of a recent or previous injury. Trotting on a leading rein may show lameness.

COAT
Check for swellings and blemishes on the back, often made by a badly fitting saddle. The coat should be clean and shiny. A dull, scaly coat is the result of parasites.

HORSE CARE

A STABLED HORSE needs constant grooming. This not only improves its looks, but also keeps the horse healthy and feeling good. Horses living in fields develop oils, giving their coat a natural gloss that can be removed by continual washing.

STABLE RUBBER

DANDY BRUSH

BODY BRUSH

WATER BRUSH

SWEAT SCRAPER

HOOF OIL AND BRUSH

HOOF PICK

METAL CURRY COMB

PLASTIC CURRY COMB

MANE COMB

SPONGE

WASH AND BRUSH UP
Stabled horses should be groomed thoroughly at least once a day. Grooming includes a number of tasks and special tools are needed to do each job properly.

CLEANING HOOVES
Clean the horse's hooves out every day using a hoof pick. This removes any matter that could collect moisture and allow germs to infect the hoof.

SPONGING THE FACE
Using water and a special sponge, clean the nose, eyes, and lips separately. Wash the sponge out thoroughly afterward.

COMBING THE TAIL
After untangling any knots, brush out the tail carefully so as not to pull out any hairs. A damp brush will flatten the short hairs at the top.

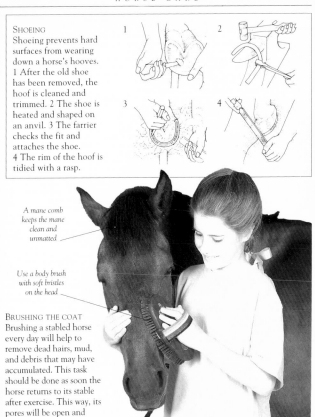

SHOEING
Shoeing prevents hard surfaces from wearing down a horse's hooves. 1 After the old shoe has been removed, the hoof is cleaned and trimmed. 2 The shoe is heated and shaped on an anvil. 3 The farrier checks the fit and attaches the shoe. 4 The rim of the hoof is tidied with a rasp.

1

2

3

4

A mane comb keeps the mane clean and unmatted

Use a body brush with soft bristles on the head

BRUSHING THE COAT
Brushing a stabled horse every day will help to remove dead hairs, mud, and debris that may have accumulated. This task should be done as soon the horse returns to its stable after exercise. This way, its pores will be open and easier to clean.

Finishing touches

Extra attention can be given to a horse if it is to be prepared for a show. After washing, the mane and tail can be braided. This also helps the mane fall in the right way later. Oiling the hooves makes them look smart. Bandages are used to protect the horse's legs when it is being transported and give it extra support and warmth during exercise. The coat can be made to look more attractive by careful clipping and combing.

1 BRAIDING A MANE
Dampen the mane and braid it in sections, starting at the top.

2 ROLLING UP
Pass a needle through the bottom of each braid and roll it up.

3 FINISHING OFF
Push needle through knot and wind thread round to hold it in place.

BRAIDING A TAIL
Start the braid at the top and gradually work down, with the ends forming a long pigtail. Secure this with an elastic band and turn it up into a loop, which is then stitched to form a double braid. Make sure it is not too tight.

Braid whole tail to the bottom of the dock.

Continue braid to the end of the tail and sew back in a double braid.

Unbraided hair hangs loose.

CLIPPING AND COMBING
The type of clip a horse receives depends on the sort of work it will do and how much it sweats. For a show, patterns may be made on a horse's rear by combing through a template in a different direction from the rest of the coat.

CHECKERBOARD COMB

OILING HOOF

Oil must not go on the hair above the hoof.

Hoof brush

CHASER CLIP

HOOF CARE
Applying hoof oil to the hoof's wall prevents it from losing moisture and becoming dry and brittle, as well as smartening its appearance. As the hoof grows, it will need trimming to prevent the wall from becoming too long and splitting.

HUNTER CLIP

1   2   3   4   5

BANDAGING LEGS
Leg bandages are wrapped over a soft lint padding. 1 Start from the top. 2 Wrap bandage in same direction as padding. 3 Finish off midway up the pastern. 4 Exercise bandage helps support the tendons. 5 Stable bandage prevents damage.

SHARK'S TEETH COMB

DRAWING A HORSE

SKETCHING OR painting a
horse is a good way to
become familiar with the
shape of its body. Practice
from pictures before drawing
a real horse, which will
move about. First, draw a
quick outline and fill in the
details later. Experiment
with different techniques,
including charcoal and
pencil. When confident, try
using some colored inks.

ARTIST'S TOOLS
You will need a set of basic
artist's tools. 1 Drawing pencil.
2 Selection of colored pencils.
3 Eraser. 4 Clipboard and paper.
5 Thick pencil. 6 Ink pen.
7 Willow charcoal. 8 Pencil
sharpener. 9 Colored inks.

DRAWING THE HEAD
The horse's face not
only reveals its breed
but can be surprisingly
expressive and full of
character. Try to
capture some of this in
your sketch. Much of
the head is made up of
small circular lines.
Rehearse a line before
actually drawing it.
Carefully mark where
short or long lines will
finish, and use these
marks as guides.

1 Begin by drawing
the outline of the
nose. These vertical
lines provide a good
reference point for the
other features.

2 As you build up the
structure of the head,
draw small, faint,
circular lines to give
overall shape to the
cheeks and eye sockets.

THE WHOLE HORSE

Try to capture the whole of the horse at a glance. Draw it quickly to suggest fluidity and agility. At first, sketch very loosely and lightly, using a pencil to get the shape of each part of the body.

1 With eyes half-closed, sketch an outline of the body and neck. Concentrate on the shape of the muscles, especially around the quarters, which will convey a sense of power.

2 Make sure the horse's hindquarters are slightly higher than the front shoulders. Then start the legs and head.

3 Look at the shapes created by the spaces between the body and legs, to help you find the correct proportions.

4 Finally, shade in the details of the body. Shadows emphasize the muscles and give the horse a solid look.

3 Complete the outline with rounded strokes to form the mane, mouth, cheek, and ears. Keep the lines light at this stage.

4 Now draw in the eyes, fetlock, and nostrils. These major features start to suggest the horse's character and expression.

5 Using the guide lines, add shading to give the head three-dimensional form. Erase any unwanted guidelines.

Resources

UNITED STATES

American Association of Equine Practitioners
4075 Iron Works Pike
Lexington, KY
40507

American Endurance Ride Conference
701 High Street
Ste 03
Auburn, CA 95603

American Horse Council
1700 K Street NW
Suite 300
Washington, DC
20006

American Horse Protection Association
1000 29th Street NW
#T-100
Washington, DC
20007

American Horse Shows Association
220 E 42nd Street,
409
New York, NY
10017

American Quarter Horse Association
P.O. Box 200
Amarillo, TX 79168

American Riding Instructor Certification Program
P.O. Box 282
Alton Bay, NH
03810

American Saddlebred Horse Association
4093 Iron Works Pike
Lexington, KY
40503

Arabian Horse Registry of America
12000 Zuni Street
Westminster, CO
80234

Coalition for Recreational Trails
3975 University Drive
Ste. 310
Fairfax, VA 22030

Harness Tracks of America Inc.
4640 East Sunrise
Ste. 200
Tucson, AZ 85718

The Jockey Club
(Thoroughbred)
821 Corporate Drive
Lexington, KY
40503

Jockey's Guild Inc. 250
West Main Street
Ste. 1820
Lexington, KY
40507

Kentucky Horse Park
4089 Iron Works Pike
Lexington, KY
40503

North American Riding for the Handicapped Association
P.O. Box 33150
Denver, CO 80233

The Professional Rodeo Cowboy's Association
101 Pro Rodeo Drive
Colorado Springs, CO 80919

Tennessee Walking Horse Breeders' and Exhibitors' Association
P.O. Box 286
Lewisburg, TN 37091

United States Dressage Federation
P.O. Box 80668
Lincoln, NE 68501

United States Trotting Association
(Standardbreds)
750 Michigan Avenue
Columbus, OH 43215

Thoroughbred Owners' and Breeders' Association
P.O. Box 4367
Lexington, KY 40544

United States Polo Association
4059 Iron Works Pike
Lexington, KY 40511

Thoroughbred Racing Association of North America
420 Fair Hill Drive
Elkton, MD 21921

United States Combined Training Association
602 South King Street
Ste 400
Leesburg, VA 22075

United States Equestrian Team
Pottersville Road
Gladstone, NJ 07934

CANADA

Breed Associations:

Canadian Thoroughbred Horse Society – National Division
P.O. Box 172 Rexdale
ON MSW 5L1

Canadian Quarter Horse Association
380-800 6th Avenue S.W.
Calgary
AB T2P 3G3

Sport Horses:

Canadian Sport Horse Association National Office
Box 520
Gormley
ON L0H 1G0

Canadian Standardbred Horse Society
2150 Meadowvale Blvd.
Mississauga
ON L5N 6R6.

Glossary

ACTION
The way a horse moves its body.

AGED
A horse of seven or more years old.

AGING
Estimating the age of a horse from its teeth.

AIDS
Signals made by the rider to communicate with the horse.

BLEMISH
Permanent mark caused by injury or disease.

BLINKERS
Flaps on the bridle to ensure the horse can only see straight ahead.

BLOOD STOCK
A racing Thoroughbred.

BLUE FEET
Blue-black coloring of the horn on the hooves of some breeds.

BONE
Circumference around the leg beneath the knee or hock, which influences the ability of the horse to carry weight. Used in the term "big boned."

BREAKING-IN
The initial training of a horse, to allow it to be ridden or harnessed.

BREED
A group bred selectively for particular features over many generations, and recognized on the basis of these characteristics.

BRIDLE
Equipment used to control a horse's head.

BROOD MARE
A mare used for breeding.

BRUSHING
A conformational fault, with the hoof or shoe striking the opposite fetlock.

BUCK
Leaping into the air: the back is kept arched, and the horse lands on its stiff forelegs.

CARRIAGE HORSE
A light horse used for pulling carriages.

CHESTNUT
The horny, oval-shaped area on the inside of the forelegs and hocks.

COLD-BLOODED
Horses with ancestors originating from the cold climates of northwestern Europe.

COLLAR
Part of a harness worn by a heavy horse for pulling loads.

COLT
Ungelded male horse under four years old.

CONFORMATION
The shape and proportions of the horse's body.

CROSSBREEDING
The mating of two horses of different breeds or types.

DAM
Mother horse.

DORSAL STRIPE
Dark hairs extending down the back toward the tail.

EQUIDAE
Family of mammals comprising all horses, ponies, asses, and zebras.

ERGOT
Horny growth located on the back of the fetlock.

FARRIER
Someone who makes horseshoes and who shoes horses.

FETLOCK
A tuft of hair that grows above a horse's hoof.

FILLY
A female horse under four years old.

FOAL
A horse under a year old.

FORELEGS
The front two legs of a horse.

FROG
The triangular-shaped pad on the bottom of the horse's foot that acts as a shock absorber.

GAIT
The way a horse moves.

GELDING
Castrated male horse.

GIRTH
Circumference of a horse's body measured from behind the withers.

HOCKS
Bones forming the knees of the rear legs.

HARNESS
Collective term for equipment used to control a draft horse.

HAUNCHES
The hips and buttocks.

HOT-BLOODED
Horses with ancestors originating from hot Middle Eastern countries.

MANE
Long hair on the back of a horse's neck.

MARTINGALE
Item of tack used to increase control of a horse's head, or to alter the pull of the reins.

MARE
A female horse more than four years old.

MULE
Offspring of a male donkey and female horse.

NEARSIDE
The left side of a horse, where it is usual to saddle-up and mount.

OFFSIDE
The right side of a horse.

PEDIGREE
The ancestry of the individual horse.

POINTS
External features, responsible for the horse's conformation.

PONY
A horse not exceeding 14.2 hh.

PUREBRED
A thoroughbred.

REINS
The strap attached to the bit.

SADDLE PAD
Pad placed under the saddle to prevent chafing or rubbing.

STALLION
An ungelded male horse over four years old.

STUD
A stallion kept for breeding.

STUD BOOK
The breed society's record, featuring the pedigrees of purebred stock.

TACK
All saddlery, riding, and driving equipment.

TYPE
A horse that fulfills a specific function, rather than a specific breed, for example, Hunter Type.

WARMBLOOD
Horses that are half- or part-bred, resulting from thoroughbred and Arabian crosses with other breeds.

WITHERS
Part of the horse above the shoulders, where the neck joins with the body.

Index

A

Africa, 18, 124, 125, 128–9, 130, 136
Akhal–Teke, 20, 78
Allenby, General, 101
American Saddlebred, 103
American Shetland, 53
Andalusian, 64, 92–3, 95
Appaloosa, 29, 90–1
Arabian, 20, 21, 86–7
  and the Australian Stock Horse, 100
  and the Boulonnais, 121
  and the Haflinger, 68
  and the Highland Pony, 54
  and the New Forest Pony, 61
  and the Percheron, 112
  and the Trakehner, 96
Ardennais, 113, 120–1
Argentina, 82–3
Asia, 18–19, 20, 91, 125
Askania–Nova Zoo, 127
Assateague, 67
asses, 124, 125, 130, 136, 137
Athena, 15
auctions, 61, 144
Australia, 41, 133, 139
Australian Pony, 62–3
Australian Stock Horse, 100–1
Austria, 68–9, 92
Auxois, 120

B

Babieca, 16
Babolna, 79
bandages, 148, 149
Barb, 21, 64, 80–1, 92, 93, 95, 112
barge horses, 16
Bavarian Warmblood, 95

Bax, 87
bay horses, 27
Baz, 87
Bedouins, 86–7
behavior, 34–5
Belgian Draft, 110–11
Belgium, 110–11, 120
Berbers, 80, 92
Bering land bridge, 19
Big Red, 43
bits, 44, 46, 47
black horses, 27
blind spot, 139
blue roan horses, 27
body, 22–3
bones, 24–5
Boulonnais, 121
Brabant, 110–11
brain, 24
branding, 28, 29
breeding, 36–7, 139
breeds, 12, 21, 139
Breton, 113
bridles, 47
Brooklyn Supreme, 110
brown horses, 27
Brumby, 133
bucking broncoes, 89
bullfighting, 93
buying a horse, 144–5

C

Caesar, Julius, 120
Camargues, 132–3
Canada, 41, 115
Cannon Ball, 64
canter, 30, 142–3
carriages, 16, 17, 69, 94
cart horses, 119
Carthusian monks, 92
Caspian, 20, 70–1, 138

cattle herding, 41, 44, 79, 101
  roping, 89
cavalry, 15, 41, 51, 78, 96
cave paintings, 13, 54
Celts, 64
ceremonial duties, 40, 41
Chapmen Horses, 95
chariots, 14, 15, 139
Charles II, Archduke, 98
chestnut horses, 26
China, 40, 42, 46, 73, 91, 107, 138
Chincoteague, 66–7
Chinook, 139
El Cid, 16
circus ponies, 55
classical riding, 45, 98–9
classification, 136–7
Cleveland Bay, 94–5
clipping, 149
Clydesdale, 55, 114–15, 138
coach horses, 96
coal mines, 51, 138
coat, 145
  colors, 26–7
  grooming, 146–9
  milk hair, 38, 39
  patterns and markings, 28–9
collars, 106, 107
Colombia, 132
Colorado Ranger, 78
colostrum, 39
colors, 26–7
Columbus, Christopher, 132
conformation, 22–3
Connemara Pony, 64–5
Cossacks, 87
cow ponies, 41
cowboys, 45, 79, 89, 139
Crimean War, 87
Criollo, 31

Crusades, 97

D
Dales Pony, 56–7
dapple gray horses, 26
Dartmoor, 58–9
Denmark, 92, 108–9, 117
diet, 32–3
digestive system, 32
diseases, 19
Dr. Le Gear, 112
domestication, 13, 14, 20
donkeys, 14, 130–1
dorsal stripe, 29
draft horses, 106–7, 119, 120
drawing, 150–1
dressage, 42, 44, 96, 103
drum horses, 115
Dülmen, 124
dun horses, 27
Dutch Courage, 103
Dutch Warmblood, 83, 102–3

E
ears, 34, 35
East European, 97
Edelweiss Pony, 69
Edinburgh, Duke of, 94
"eel" stripes, 55
Egypt, ancient, 14, 71, 139
Elizabeth II, Queen, 95
endurance riding, 87
English Cart Horse, 119
Eohippus, 18, 19
Equidae, 136–7
equipment, 46–7, 140, 146
Europe, 18, 20, 46, 91
evolution, 18–19
Exmoor, 20, 58–9
eyes, 23, 59, 139, 145

F
face markings, 28
Falabella, 72–3
Falabella, Julio Cesar, 73

farming, 40, 107, 111, 114–15, 116, 120–1, 139
farriers, 147
feathering, 106, 109
Fell Pony, 56–7
feral horses, 124–5, 132–3
Firouz, Louise L., 70
Flanders Horse, 111
fleabitten horses, 26
flehmening, 34
foals, 13
  development, 36–7
  food, 32–3
  growing up, 38–9
  proportions, 12
food, 32–3
Forest Horse, 121
forestry, 40, 41, 107
France, 112–13, 120–1, 131, 132
freeze marks, 29
Friesian, 56, 81

G
gaits, 30
gallop, 30, 142–3
Galway, 64
Gelderlander, 103
Genghis Khan, 139
Germany, 96–7, 124
Gobi Desert, 127
grass, 32
gray horses, 26
Great Horses, 118
Greece, ancient, 15
Grevy's zebras, 128, 137
Groningen, 103
grooming, 34, 146–9

H
Hackney Pony, 57
Hadrian's Wall, 56
Haflinger, 68–9
Hamilton, 6th duke of, 115
harness racing, 78

hay, 33
heavy horses, 21, 31, 105–21
herbivores, 12, 32
herding cattle, 41, 44, 79, 101
herds, 13, 34, 124, 133
Highland Pony, 54–5
hinnies, 14, 130–1
Hipparion, 18
Hittites, 139
holidays, 42, 43
hooves, 12, 145
  cleaning, 146
  markings, 29
  oiling, 148, 149
  ponies, 51
  shoeing, 147
Horse Type 1 and 2, 20
Hoshaba, 87
Household Cavalry, 115
Hungary, 79
hunting, 15
hybrids, 136

I
Icelandic Horse, 74–5
identity markings, 29
incisor teeth, 33
India, 40, 41
insects, 139
Iran, 70–1, 125, 138
Ireland, 64–5, 130
Irish Hobby, 64
Italian Heavy Horse, 107
Italy, 45, 107

J
jaws, 33
Jerez de la Frontera, 92, 93
jockeys, 46
jodhpurs, 47, 140
jousting, 16–17
jumping, 31, 42, 142
Jutland, 108–9, 117

K
Kadesh, battle of, 139
Kentucky Horse Park, 43, 102
keratin, 12
knights, 16–17, 44, 47, 96, 108, 118
Koran, 87
Kulan asses, 125, 137

L
Lascaux, 54
legs, 22–3, 145
  bandaging, 148, 149
  ligaments and tendons, 25
  markings, 29
  movements, 30–1
leisure, 42–3
life cycle, 36–7
lifespan, 36
ligaments, 25
light horses, 21, 31, 77–103
Lipizzaner, 45, 98–9
Little Pumpkin, 138
liver chestnut horses, 26
Lusitano, 81

M
Man O'War, 43
manes, 13, 139, 148
Marengo, 87
mares, 34, 36
markings, 28–9
mating, 36
Maud, 139
Medusa, 15
Merlin, 62
Merychippus, 19
Mesohippus, 18
Middle East, 131
Mierfelder Bruch, 124
milk hair, 38, 39
Milton, 103
miniature horses, 72–3, 138
Miniature Shetland, 52
Miohippus, 18

Missouri Fox Trotter, 78
Misty of Chincoteague, 67
Mix, Tom, 139
molars, 33
Mongols, 139
Monleki, 70
Moors, 80, 112
Morgan, 102–3
Morgan, Justin, 103
Mountain zebras, 128, 137
mounting, 141
movement, 30–1
mules, 40, 130–1, 136
muscles, 24–5
Mustangs, 133

N
Napoleon I, Emperor, 87, 121
Native Americans, 84, 90
neck, 22–3
Netherlands, 83
New Forest Pony, 60–1, 124
Newmarket, 83
Newton, 73
Nez Percé tribe, 90
Noah, 87
Noriker, 68
Norman Cob, 113
North Africa, 80–1, 92, 112
North America, 18–19, 41, 72, 78–9
Northern Ireland, 139
Norway, 74, 75
Norwegian Fjord, 75
nose, 145
Nourouzabad stud, 70

O
Olympic Games, 96, 139
onagers, 14, 125, 137
Overo, 85

P
paces, 30–1, 142–3
pack ponies, 16, 57, 58, 64, 69

paint horse, 85
Palio, Siena, 43
Palomino, 26, 79, 84–5, 139
Palomino, Juan de, 84
Palouse valley, 91
Paterson, John, 115
patterns and markings, 28–9
Pegasus, 15
Pennines, 56
Percheron, 54, 112–13
Perissodactyla, 136
Persian empire, 15, 42
phaetons, 17
Piber, 99
piebald horses, 27
Pinto, 84f5
pit ponies, 51, 138
Plains zebras, 128–9
Pliohippus, 19
plowing, 107, 111, 114, 115
points of the horse, 22–3
poisonous plants, 33
police horses, 40, 41
polo, 42, 43, 51, 138
ponies, 21, 31, 49–75
Ponseki, 70
Pony Express, 138
Pony Type 1 and 2, 20
pregnancy, 36–7
proportions, 12, 23
Przewalski, Colonel N.M., 126–7
Przewalski's Horse, 20, 80, 126–7, 137

Q
quaggas, 129
Quarter Horse, 41, 88–9

R
racing, 42–3, 139
  harness, 78
  Quarter Horse, 88
  racehorses, 43, 65
  Thoroughbreds, 82–3